Susan Blackwell, Gideon Glick, Sarah Steele and Jason Fuchs in a scene from the
Roundabout Theatre Company production of *Speech & Debate*.

SPEECH & DEBATE

BY STEPHEN KARAM

★ Revised Edition

★

DRAMATISTS
PLAY SERVICE
INC.

ACKNOWLEDGMENTS

This play was born out of the generous dramaturgical/creative support and talents of many people; Lowry Marshall for agreeing to workshop the play before I even finished it; Sarah Coogan, Anne Reilly, Patricia Mcgregor, Will Rogers, Chris Burney, Jason Moore; all of the actors listed in the first two productions; Ellen Langan and Agnes Cummings for their Scranton High School Speech & Debate coaching genius; Robyn Goodman for believing in the piece and making it happen; Chris Till for setting everything in motion; Darius, Kerry and Sam for introducing me to the great state of Oregon; all the folks at Roundabout: Julia Levy, Harold Wolpert, Rebecca Habel, Jill Rafson, Josh Fielder; and Todd Haimes, for his generous and enthusiastic support throughout the entire process.

Special thanks to Mary Rodgers, Bill Gaden and all the good people at the Rodgers & Hammerstein Organization for seeing the play and not shutting it down. All *S&D* vocals are now and forever for you, Mary.

SPEECH & DEBATE was originally performed as a workshop production at Brown/Trinity Playwrights Repertory Theatre (Lowry Marshall, Artistic Director) in Providence, Rhode Island, in July 2006. It was directed by Lowry Marshall and the production stage manager was Robyn Grady. The cast was as follows:

HOWIE .... Justin Blanchard
SOLOMON .... Steven Levenson
DIWATA .... Lucy DeVito
TEACHER ....Darius Pierce
REPORTER .... Crystal Finn

SPEECH & DEBATE received its world premiere at Roundabout Theatre Company (Todd Haimes, Artistic Director) as the inaugural production of Roundabout Underground in New York City, opening in October 2007. It was directed by Jason Moore; the set design was by Anna Louizos; the costume design was by Heather Dunbar; the lighting design was by Justin Townsend; the sound and projection design were by Brett Jarvis; the choreography was by Boo Killabrew; Howie's and Solomon's art was by Lowry Marshall and Steven Levenson; the original music was composed by Stephen Karam; and the production stage managers were James Fitzsimmons and Cyrille Blackburn. The cast was as follows:

HOWIE .... Gideon Glick
SOLOMON .... Jason Fuchs
DIWATA .... Sarah Steele
TEACHER/REPORTER .... Susan Blackwell

SPEECH & DEBATE was subsequently produced at American Theatre Company in Chicago, Illinois, in April 2008. It was directed by PJ Paparelli; the set design was by Keith Pitts; the costume design was by Myron Elliott; the lighting design was by Charles Cooper; the sound design was by Scotty Iseri and Lindsay Jones; the video/projection design was by Marty Higginbotham and Bobby Richards; the choreography was by Ed Kross; the original music was composed by Stephen Karam; and the production stage manager was Dana Nestrick. The cast was as follows:

HOWIE ....Patrick Andrews
SOLOMON .... Jared McGuire
DIWATA ....Sadieh Rifai
TEACHER/REPORTER .... Cheryl Graeff

SCENE BREAKDOWN

Scene titles should be projected at the start of each scene.

SCENE 1: Poetry Reading

SCENE 2: Lincoln-Douglas Debate

SCENE 3: Extemporaneous Commentary

SCENE 4: Storytelling

SCENE 5: Dramatic/Humorous Interpretation

SCENE 6: Cross-Examination Debate

SCENE 7: Duo Interpretation

SCENE 8: Declamation

SCENE 9: Group Interpretation

SCENE 10: Oral Interpretation of Prose*

SCENE 11: Student Congress

SCENE 12: Original Oratory

AUTHOR'S NOTE

*Scene 10 was included in the original New York production; it was cut in subsequent productions. The show may be performed without it at the producing theater's discretion.

A slash (/) indicates the point of overlap in dialogue. Wherever the slash (/) appears, the character with the next line of dialogue begins their speech.

CHARACTERS

SOLOMON, 16

DIWATA, 17

HOWIE, 18

TEACHER/REPORTER, 40s — female; the Teacher and Reporter could (I think should) be played by one actress. These adult roles are not caricatures — so obviously, they shouldn't be played as such. The Teacher and Reporter have good intentions — they are never (intentionally) snide.

PLACE

Salem, Oregon.

"Children should not be asked to touch anyone in the areas of their body that would be covered by a bathing suit or allow anyone to touch them in those areas."

— Sheriff's Office, Marion County, Oregon

dannyboy:	what do you like about youth?
therightbi-guy:	energy,
therightbi-guy:	wonder,
dannyboy:	personally i like the tight ass
dannyboy:	lol
dannyboy:	but thats just me
dannyboy:	lol
therightbi-guy:	their hopes for the future. and their whole life in front of them
dannyboy:	so their innocence?
therightbi-guy:	no, i don't think. i didn't think of you as an innocent
dannyboy:	thats good … cuz i'm not

—from a transcript of an online chat, dated November 30, 2004, between the former mayor of Spokane, WA, Jim West ("therightbi-guy"), and an 18-year-old male ("dannyboy").

SPEECH & DEBATE

Scene 1: Poetry Reading

The stage should be relatively spare, dominated by a large screen or back wall onto which various images can be projected.

With a loud tympani crash, there is a total blackout.

Lights up on an 18-year-old boy, Howie. He has his computer keyboard in his lap and is in the middle of an instant message chat.

Howie's screen name is "BlBoi;" the unseen stranger he is communicating with is "BiGuy." Their names appear on the screen in two different colors.

The dialogue's projection is timed precisely with the music from Aaron Copland's "Fanfare for the Common Man."* The result is a choreographed musical number. A cyber-ballet.

BIGUY:	im scared
BLBOI:	y?
BIGUY:	u r 2 young
BLBOI:	says who?
BIGUY:	the police

(Howie searches for clip art on his computer, finds a picture, pastes it, presses return.)

BLBOI:	*[image of a crying baby]*
BIGUY:	LOL

* See Special Note on Songs and Recordings on copyright page and Production Notes on page 69.

BLBOI:	Im 18
	Blonde
	Smooth
	Lean
	Legal
BIGUY:	You're of age?
BLBOI:	in OR
BIGUY:	Are you sure?
BLBOI:	yessiree
BIGUY:	:)
BLBOI:	:)
BIGUY:	I like you
BLBOI:	U like youth
	right?
BIGUY:	Yes
BLBOI:	Why?
BIGUY:	Hmmmmmm …
	Energy
	Wonder
	Optimism
BLBOI:	Tight ass
BIGUY:	LOL
BLBOI:	LOL
BIGUY:	ROFL
BLBOI:	ROFL?
BIGUY:	Rolling on the floor laughing

(Howie makes sure no one is outside his door.)

BIGUY:	im 36

(Howie reacts, disappointed.)

BIGUY:	That 2 old?
BLBOI:	Not 2 old …
BIGUY:	… but …
BLBOI:	R
	U
	Generu$?
BIGUY:	Send a pic

(Howie searches for clip art on his computer, finds a picture, pastes it, presses return.)

BLBOI:	*[image of a six-year-old boy at a computer keyboard]*
BIGUY:	not funny.

(Howie poses, takes a picture of himself shirtless in time with the music.) [Snap, flash.] (He takes another picture.) [Snap, flash.] (He returns to the computer.)

BLBOI:	Whats yur job?
BIGUY:	I cant say
	Im discrete
BLBOI:	Closet case
BIGUY:	:(
BLBOI:	Priest?
BIGUY:	No
BLBOI:	Pope?
BIGUY:	Yes
BLBOI:	That's hot
BIGUY:	Will wear my pointy hat
	When u visit the vatican
BLBOI:	LOL
BIGUY:	Meet me now
BLBOI:	Where?
BIGUY.	Riverfront Park
BLBOI:	When?
BIGUY:	Midnight
BLBOI:	K
BIGUY:	Send your pic
	to
	dramedy@aol.com

(Howie is shocked upon seeing the email address. He stands up, nervous. The tympani roll at the end of the song climaxes with a blackout.)

Scene 2: Lincoln/Douglas Debate

Lights up on Solomon, 16. He stands with a few loose-leaf papers in hand. He is speaking with a female teacher. She is gathering her belongings, getting ready to leave.

SOLOMON. Why can't I write about abortion?

TEACHER. This is the principal's decision, Solomon. It's too controversial, parents complain every time without fail —

SOLOMON. But isn't that the point of the school paper, to create a forum for students to discuss issues actually affecting us? Why ban the most controversial issues?

TEACHER. Abortion is the only topic that is off-limits.

SOLOMON. How about religion?

TEACHER. You can't write about religion.

SOLOMON. Why not?

TEACHER. Separation of church and state, you know this. Other than that, the principal has been very clear: no abortion op-eds. No pro-choice pieces, no pro-life pieces. I'm sorry.

SOLOMON. What about an article about the mayor?

TEACHER. That would be fine.

SOLOMON. And how he's had sex with teenagers? *(Teacher sighs, Solomon takes out a newspaper.)* It's in today's *Statesman Journal*, have you read it?

TEACHER. I've glanced at the headlines.

SOLOMON. Our fifty-five-year-old mayor has had sex with three teenage boys.

TEACHER. The facts are not known —

SOLOMON. The facts are that he's a right-wing Republican, an opponent of gay rights, and is now accused of having secret online relationships with several teenage boys.

TEACHER. These stories take time to unfold, we won't know the truth for some time —

SOLOMON. Which is why my article is more about the pattern I've discovered, a —

TEACHER. A pattern?

SOLOMON. A pattern of Republican politicians — I've been researching this on the internet — even in the last few years alone —

TEACHER. You sound as if you've already started writing this, you never received my approval —

SOLOMON. *(Reading from his notes.)* In 2004 — just let me read this bit — David Dreier, twelve-term Republican congressman who voted for a measure that banned gays from adopting in Washington, D.C., is revealed to be, surprise, living with a man —

TEACHER. Solomon, I'm not sure what —

SOLOMON. — 2006, Mark Foley is texting pages in the Capitol building — which, any idiot should know those files will be stored in your cache —   TEACHER.
And no one's learning any lessons,   Your what — ?
there's Ed Schrock, Ted Haggard —

TEACHER. Can you wrap it up, please —

SOLOMON. — Larry Craig, Bob Allen, he's my favorite, Florida co-chairman of the McCain campaign. The man introduced legislation to outlaw people from quote "intentionally masturbating" in public, and — *(Quick aside to Teacher.)* — as opposed to *accidentally* masturbating? — *(Back to notes.)* — he then gets caught in a bathroom offering a police officer *twenty bucks for a blowjob*! —

TEACHER. Okay —

SOLOMON. — and now it's happening right here in Salem — our mayor has opposed every bit of gay rights legislation proposed in Oregon and yet —

TEACHER. Slow down, first of all, you're making these issues uniquely Republican, you could easily research similar Democratic scandals, President Clinton —

SOLOMON. — but people expect that kind of behavior from Democrats —

TEACHER. Solomon —

SOLOMON. — I'm just saying, my piece is exploring the phenomenon of *Republican conservatives*, politicians who spend their careers championing morality, American values, *the sanctity of marriage* — people like our mayor, Congressman Foley, Rick Santorum, who —

TEACHER. Rick Santorum isn't gay —

SOLOMON. Well, not yet, but the pattern —

TEACHER. You're trying to cause a stir, and I —

SOLOMON. I'm trying to figure out how a man can make the decision to live a fictional life *so fully* that he becomes capable of *publicly* pushing policy that cuts against … who he is.

TEACHER. Have you talked to your parents about this?

SOLOMON. No, they think I'm writing about abortion. This topic would be too controversial for them. *(Beat.)*

TEACHER. Right, well … the fact that you don't feel comfortable speaking to your parents about your new topic … maybe that's what *I'm* feeling …

SOLOMON. You need to read this to appreciate how good this is, there's / — hold on …

TEACHER. Solomon, please …

SOLOMON. The editor of the newspaper confronts our mayor and asks … *(Reading from the paper.)* "Mr. Mayor, why don't you just come clean and tell me that being gay is part of who you are. We have several transcripts from gay.com in which you admit to your fondness for young men." *(To Teacher.)* But the amazing thing is, the mayor refuses to come out. Even after being caught, even after all of the evidence, the mayor says: *(Reading.)* "I am a straight man who likes to mentor kids." On *gay.com*?

TEACHER. Solomon, *enough*.

SOLOMON. Are you mad because you supported his campaign?

TEACHER. Excuse me?

SOLOMON. I have a program here from a fundraising dinner listing you as a sponsor for the mayor's county initiative. *(Beat.)* You're listed under "fifty dollars or less." *(Beat.)* I googled you. *(Solomon takes out a tape recorder.)*

TEACHER. What are you doing? Have you been tape-recording me?

SOLOMON. Yes. I have a release form here for you to sign. At the end of our talk. If you don't mind.

TEACHER. I'm not signing anything. Why would I sign something? And please turn that off.

SOLOMON. But you did support his campaign?

TEACHER. What? That has absolutely nothing to do with my disapproving your topic. And please *turn that off.*

SOLOMON. Are you a Log Cabin Republican?

TEACHER. Am I — what?

SOLOMON. The *Oregonian* says he's the first Republican mayor in fifteen years to lose the backing of the Salem chapter of that group, / I'm wondering why —

TEACHER. No, of course I'm not. I'm not even — of course I'm not —

SOLOMON. You're not what? What is a Log Cabin Republican?

TEACHER. You know what, why don't you ask your parents.

SOLOMON. I'll google it.

TEACHER. Google it, then. Good.

SOLOMON. I know you're not a lesbian.

TEACHER. Solomon!

SOLOMON. I'm just saying, why would I have to ask my parents? Why can't we talk about anything real in school? Why is everybody so nervous?

TEACHER. *Turn the recorder off.*

SOLOMON. I'm sorry. *(He turns it off.)* I'm thinking of writing a separate, bigger piece about freedom of speech in high schools. If it's good I can have my dad pitch it to his friend who works at *The Oregonian*. My dad's a lawyer, he knows tons of people.

TEACHER. Is this why you keep choosing controversial subjects? So I can reject them and fuel your story?

SOLOMON. No.

TEACHER. Because your father was one of the parents who complained to the principal about some of the topics the paper has published this year. I thought you were aware of this. *(Beat.)*

SOLOMON. No. He didn't — no, I didn't know ... I can't believe he talked to you ...

TEACHER. Talk to your parents about this. Please.

SOLOMON. Everyone always says that, "talk to your parents," "ask your parents" — why can't we talk about these things in school?

TEACHER. The school district has several forums — there are at least three assemblies every year —

SOLOMON. Yes, I know — have you ever sat in on one of them? There's the stranger-danger session where we are told by some experts not to let anyone touch us in our bathing suit areas. That's what they say. Our *bathing suit areas*. Half of our class is having real-life sex and — I'm not, but — and they're talking to us about our bathing suit areas? Our *bathing suit areas*? Why don't they talk about stuff we actually want to know about, like how do you actually *do* oral sex and —

TEACHER. Okay, time's up, / I'm sorry —

SOLOMON. I'm going to write this story. *(Beat.)*

TEACHER. Have you considered finding another outlet for all of this energy? What about Speech & Debate? It's a brand new activity for us — next year there will be a faculty advisor to start up the first team.

SOLOMON. No, I don't like public speaking, you're trying to change the subject —

TEACHER. Miss Langan is looking for a student volunteer to learn about the different events; someone to raise student interest now so that the club can hit the ground running next year.

SOLOMON. Every morning when it's announced people laugh, everyone thinks it's a joke.

TEACHER. You should at least learn about the different events —

SOLOMON. I'll google it …

TEACHER. Google it, then, good. *(Solomon starts to put his tape recorder away.)*

SOLOMON. So do you have any other comments? Clarifications before we end the interview?

TEACHER. It's not an interview, and if you use any of my quotes out of context, I'll personally escort you to the principal's office. *(Beat. Solomon still has the tape recorder in his hand.)*

SOLOMON. I could write an article about how Abraham Lincoln was a homosexual.

TEACHER. Solomon!

SOLOMON. In civics class, you told us —

TEACHER. No, I did not! You asked me if — I mentioned in passing that several historians — I never, I *stressed* that there is no evidence to — and — Solomon, is that tape recorder on? …

SOLOMON. Was I supposed to keep it off?

TEACHER. Yes!

	SOLOMON.
Just, okay, just let me speak to the principal, okay? Let's see what Miss Langan says and I'll get back to you. Okay? *(Beat. Solomon smiles.)*	Sorry, sorry …

SOLOMON. Thank you. *(Blackout.)*

Scene 3: Extemporaneous Commentary

Diwata's bedroom. A Casio keyboard and four empty wine coolers are on the floor.

She pushes the "playback" button on her keyboard.

A few chords sound, playing over and over. She checks her computer, picks up the microphone attached to it and begins to sing.

Her opening verse is more mellow and melancholy than loud and showy.

DIWATA.
Sittin' at my Casio keyboard
Thank God it's built to pre-record
Otherwise I couldn't play and sing
At the same time

I'm ...

Sittin' at my Casio keyboard
Kinda drunk and
Really fuckin' bored
Otherwise I'd have better things to do
Than update my blog

On a Friday night
(Diwata has some more to drink.) Welcome to the first podcast entry of my diary, updated daily at monoblog.com. Let's hear it for my band — that's Casio in the background. Casio's been programmed to play the only three chords I know over and over while I improvise a new song, live, before your ears, America. Ideally, the music would be a little more interesting, but I can't play and sing at the same time, and I have no friends to help me out. "But Diwata," you're saying to

yourselves, "You're so odd and frumpy — you must have friends." But no, I don't. All I have is my music. *(Singing, improvising.)*

There is music in my body.

(She turns her keyboard off.) Nice. The upcoming auditions for this year's spring musical were the inspiration for this live, streaming musical entry. My high school will be doing the timeless classic *Once Upon a Mattress*, and this year, like every other year, I will not get cast because of my talentless drama teacher — a man I'll call gay-guy-with-a-receding-hairline in order to protect Mr. Walter M. Healy's anonymity. But this year, I think *America* should decide whether or not I get to showcase my skills in North Salem High's multipurpose room. "But Diwata," you're asking, "How can we show you our undying love?" Calm yourselves, I'll tell you. You see, Mr. Healy was foolish enough to include his email address on the bottom of his class syllabus; so I say, let the e-campaign begin: if you think that I should play the lead in the spring play, write to the fool at dramedy@aol.com. That's D-R-A-M-E-D-Y at A-O-L.com. *(She turns the keyboard on, starting the musical vamp.)* Mr. Healy, this verse ... is for you. *(Singing.)*

Mr. Healy you're a crap sandwich
I'm pure and you're a crap sandwich
Get some bread, your balding head, and some more bread
You have your head between bread
Crap sandwich ... yeah ...

(Pleased with her work.) Fierce. I totally improv'd that. That's right — what you heard was free-form, free-flow, yo ho, yo ho but I know some people listening are gonna go, "Maybe it's Miss Monoblog who's the freak," they're saying. Well, I happen to know first-hand that it's Mr. Healy who's got problems ... Let's just say our fine mayor isn't the only one keeping secrets ... but if you still think Miss Monoblog is just a crazy drama queen, allow me to share a brief story with you that will clear all this up. *(Diwata stops the musical vamp.)* At Friday's drama club meeting, Mr. Healy proudly announced that he will be altering the plot of our spring musical, *Once Upon a Mattress*, ever so slightly to make it more appropriate for the needs of our conservative community. Lady Larkin, the character who needs to get married ASAP because she is pregnant out of wedlock, will no longer be pregnant. That's right — to avoid the raciness of an unwed mom, Lady Larkin will just really, *really* want to get married. We have a *teen mothers program* at our high

school, and the man thinks an unwed mother is too racy for us? *(Diwata starts the musical vamp again, rallying the troops.)* Are we in Salem, Oregon or Salem, Massachusetts circa sixteen-twenty-whenever-those-witches-were-bein'-hunted? *(Singing.)*

> *Well you can't burn me*
> *This witch is fireproof*
> *So try and hang me*
> *And see how strong my neck is*

Bold. That's an excerpt from "Headstrong," a ballad from my new original musical *Crucible*, based on Arthur Miller's play *The Crucible*. The show is told entirely from the perspective of Mary Warren, a part I was born to play, and a part I was denied last year by the man who shall remain nameless, Mr. Walter M. Healy. Currently, *Crucible* is on hiatus until I rewrite the plot or until Arthur fucking Miller's estate agrees to release the rights to me. Whatever. *(Singing.)*

> *Try to burn me*
> *But you'll be dead wrong*
> *You can try to hang me*
> *But this girl is headstrong*

(She turns the music off.) Wicked. Enough about me. Right now, I'm worried about the composer of *Once Upon a Mattress*, Mary Rodgers. Because once she hears about Mr. Healy's heinous changes, she will die. And if she's already dead, she will karate kick her way out of her coffin to find Mr. Healy and slap him in the balls. *(She starts the musical vamp.)* And so, an impromptu dirge for Miss Mary ... *(Singing.)*

> *Oh ... oh ...*

(Lights up on Howie and Solomon in front of their computers in their bedrooms. They are listening to Diwata's podcast.)

> *All the guys sing ...*

DIWATA and HOWIE.

> *Oh ... oh ...*

DIWATA.

> And all the ladies go ...

DIWATA and SOLOMON.

> *Oh-ee ... oh-ee ... oh-ee ... oh-ee ... oh-ee ... oh-ee ...*
> *Oh ... whoa ... oh ...*

HOWIE. *(Simultaneously with the above.)*

> *Oh ... oh ...*

(All three now sing their own parts together.)

21

Oh ... oh ...

SOLOMON. *(Simultaneously with the above.)*
Oh-ee ... oh-ee ... oh-ee ... oh-ee ... oh-ee ... oh-ee ... oh ...
Whoa ... oh ...

DIWATA. *(Simultaneously with Howie and Solomon.)*
Sittin' at my Casio keyboard
Thank God it's built to pre-record
Otherwise I couldn't play and sing
At the same time
I'm —

(The following three voices all overlap.)

VOICE (DIWATA'S MOTHER). Diwata, that is the most annoying thing I've ever heard in my life.

VOICE (SOLOMON'S FATHER). Solomon, what are you doing? Are you *singing?*

VOICE (HOWIE'S MOTHER). I'm trying to sleep, Howie, please ... *(Beat. All three are embarrassed.)*

DIWATA. We're having technical difficulties, so I leave you with this: Lady Larkin and I have a lot in common. We aren't both perfectly pretty, and I don't have Lady Larkin's perfect soprano voice. But we had something in common until you messed everything up. *(She feels her stomach.)* Fuck you, Mr. Healy. *(Lights shift, focus on Howie, who is busy typing. His message is projected on the screen. It reads: "liked your blog entry. Have my own dirt on Healy. yur right — mayor isn't the only one keeping secrets. Call me. 503 555 4756 — message posted by BlBoi@ aol.com at 7:58PM." Blackout.)*

Scene 4: Storytelling

In the blackout we hear a phone ring. Howie picks up the call.

HOWIE. Hello?

SOLOMON. Hi, I'm looking for the person who owns the screen-name "B-L Boy"? It's an AOL screenname. "Boy" is spelled "B-O-I."

HOWIE. Who is this?

SOLOMON. I'm a reporter, from *The Trojan*. I just read a post on a website called monoblog.com — it listed this phone number. The post read: "Got my own dirt on Healy. yur right — mayor isn't the only one keeping secrets."

HOWIE. I didn't realize my post was public, sorry. I posted it for the girl who did that podcast —

SOLOMON. I'm working on a story for *The Trojan* involving the mayor's sex scandal. I'd like to interview you.

HOWIE. Why do you want to interview *me*?

SOLOMON. Your message implies that Mr. Healy has also had relationships with younger guys, like the mayor. That might be newsworthy. He *is* a high school / teacher.

HOWIE. Wait, is *The Trojan* — is that the *school* / paper?

SOLOMON. Don't hang up, please. I just want to find out what you know about Mr. Healy. Can you tell me —

HOWIE. No, sorry —

SOLOMON. I know you think I'm not a real reporter, but I have lots of experience, I've already won some awards.

HOWIE. Like what kind of experience? What kind of awards?

SOLOMON. Like, there's a few things, like, honorable mention in the National Write and Illustrate Your Own Book Contest / and I'm —

HOWIE. I got third place in that contest when I was in fifth grade. Isn't it only open to younger / kids only…?

SOLOMON. If you'd let me finish … I'm the first sophomore to become an associate editor of *The Trojan* —

HOWIE. … and isn't it called the *Oregon* Write and Illustrate Your Own Book Contest? It's not national. Why should I talk to you? —

SOLOMON. Because you posted a private message to a public bulletin board, and I read it. And I can direct anyone to that website, including Mr. Healy or real reporters who will cover the story and find out your secret whether you want them to or not.

HOWIE. *(Angrily.)* Dude, relax, okay? Don't do that, don't be a freak. *Please ...*

SOLOMON. I won't, I'm sorry. *(Beat.)*

HOWIE. So ... goodbye. Okay? *(Beat.)*

SOLOMON. What was your story about?

HOWIE. What?

SOLOMON. You said you got third place, so I'm just asking —

HOWIE. What? Why the hell / would you ask —

SOLOMON. You don't have to tell me if —

HOWIE. I'm not going to tell you. Goodbye, okay?

SOLOMON. Tell me or I'll call Mr. Healy. *(Howie is pissed off. Holds the phone away from him. He's unsure what to do.)* What was it about? *(Beat.)* Are you there? *(Beat.)*

HOWIE. *(Holding back his anger.)* It was about this kid who travels back in time.

SOLOMON. How far back?

HOWIE. Very far back, to like, Biblical times, okay?

SOLOMON. Like in a time machine? How does he do that?

HOWIE. I don't remember. Goodbye, okay?

SOLOMON. Who does he meet? / What does he do?

HOWIE. Jesus Christ ... he meets some other guy, Cain.

SOLOMON. Like, Cain from the Bible?

HOWIE. You don't know when you read it, but it's Biblical times, so you figure it out.

SOLOMON. What happens to Cain?

HOWIE. Why do you care?

SOLOMON. Tell me.

HOWIE. Or what?

SOLOMON. Or ... I might call Mr. Healy. *(Beat. Howie is angry. He collects himself, proceeds ...)*

HOWIE. Cain is like, totally put off by how queeny the time-travel kid is.

SOLOMON. The time-travel kid is queeny? How would people know that?

HOWIE. My illustrations ... *(Projection of one of Howie's illustrations: A picture of a masculine Cain, perhaps with a club, disapproving of a modern queeny kid. It is well-drawn for a ten-year-old.)*

SOLOMON. Okay, okay — so then what? What does the queeny kid do?

HOWIE. I told you, he time travels.

SOLOMON. And he meets Cain?

HOWIE. Yes.

SOLOMON. And ... they do — what do they do?

HOWIE. Nothing, Cain hates him. So he goes to kill him.

SOLOMON. The queeny kid? Why would Cain kill the queeny kid?

HOWIE. Because he's pissed off that this kid is all gay and queeny, and Cain wants him dead.

SOLOMON. Okay, okay, that's abrupt, but okay ...

HOWIE. And right before Cain strikes him down, the kid whispers in his ear ... *(Projection: Illustration of the queeny kid whispering in Cain's ear.)* "Your brother is just like me."

SOLOMON. What does that mean?

HOWIE. *(Obviously.)* It means Cain's brother is gay ...

SOLOMON. Abel? Abel is gay? How would the queeny kid know that?

HOWIE. Gaydar, I don't remember. I was nine.

SOLOMON. Okay, okay ... and then ... and then, what?

HOWIE. Cain kills the kid. *(Projection: Cain standing over a bloody queeny kid.)* And then Cain kills his brother. *(Projection: Cain standing over two bloody queeny kids.)* The end.

SOLOMON. So this is confusing. You changed the Bible story? So that Cain really killed Abel because Abel was gay?

HOWIE. Yes.

SOLOMON. That is so confusing ... and you got third place? ...

HOWIE. *(Howie smiles in disbelief at Solomon's seriousness.)* It's pretty messed up because I wrote it when I was nine, right after I came out.

SOLOMON. You came out when you were nine?

HOWIE. Yeah — well, ten officially.

SOLOMON. So why isn't your time-travel kid in the Bible? How do you explain that?

HOWIE. Are you really this serious?

SOLOMON. What?

HOWIE. Nevermind. Are we done?

SOLOMON. I'm not serious.

HOWIE. Okay ...

SOLOMON. Why would you say that? — You act like — / What is that …

HOWIE. Wow, you're a freak.

SOLOMON. I'm not a freak. I'm just not serious in some bad way.

HOWIE. Really?

SOLOMON. Yeah …

HOWIE. Good for you.

SOLOMON. Yeah, good for me.

HOWIE. *(Smiling.)* I bet your *story* was serious.

SOLOMON. Not in a bad way, no. Actually, it was historical fiction/action-adventure, actually.

HOWIE. Oh yeah?

SOLOMON. Yeah.

HOWIE. Good. So have I answered all your / questions? —

SOLOMON. It was about this kid, Abraham Lincoln —

HOWIE. No, I don't need to know / this —

SOLOMON. No, I know — but he's a teenager in my story, though, like fourteen, I'm just saying, which was kind of creative to write about Abraham Lincoln as a boy since most people think of him as a man that's all I'm saying. So —

HOWIE. Did he have like acne, how did you draw him young?

SOLOMON. No, I studied historical portraits from the period. *(Projection: Solomon's illustration of a very poorly drawn [borderline stick-figure] teenage Abe Lincoln.)* And it's basically about teenage Abraham Lincoln meeting this girl in the library in his town, and the girl hates to read and learn … and over the course of this rainy day, he teaches her to love reading and love learning. *(Projection: An illustration of poorly-drawn teenage Abe Lincoln with poorly-drawn girl in town. The girl looks very boyish, wearing overalls. They hold hands.)* Because he really did love those things in real life, it was based on, on his real … oh my God, my story sucks. *(The projection fades out.)*

HOWIE. Yeah.

SOLOMON. It's really terrible, isn't it? I mean I was only eleven, but —

HOWIE. I wouldn't worry about it.

SOLOMON. No, I'm not worried about it. I'm not *worried* about it.

HOWIE. Good.

SOLOMON. Very good. *(Beat.)* So, goodbye, I guess.

HOWIE. Yeah — and you're not going to call Mr. —

SOLOMON. I won't do that, no.

HOWIE. Thank you —

SOLOMON. Have you won other awards besides that third place? —

HOWIE. What? / Oh my God …

SOLOMON. It's a simple question.

HOWIE. Why do you care? / You're such a freak —

SOLOMON. You *haven't* won any other awards …

HOWIE. Uh, let me see … I was an Eagle Scout at fifteen. That was good. I haven't cured cancer or anything.

SOLOMON. I thought you couldn't be a Boy Scout if you were, you know —

HOWIE. No — well, I mean this one time I even made up a dance for a Scout talent show, like an actual dance I choreographed to George Michael's "Freedom." So, maybe they didn't know, but I mean … *that* was gay.

SOLOMON. What kind of dance?

HOWIE. It wasn't a *kind* of dance, I just had all these special moves I made up, that I was going to teach to everybody —

SOLOMON. What made them special? What were your moves?

HOWIE. They weren't really special, I made them up in my bedroom so, you know, they were my moves, that's all I mean.

SOLOMON. Okay, I'm with you, and then …

HOWIE. Then what?

SOLOMON. Did they like your moves, what?

HOWIE. That's not the point.

SOLOMON. They *didn't* like your moves — ?

HOWIE. *I didn't do them*, why do you ask so many questions, you're / such a freak …

SOLOMON. Why didn't you do them?

HOWIE. Because I got there and the other guys were doing all this shit, tying knots, throwing curveballs … The kid before me did some lame wrestling moves, how to pin someone or something — *of course I didn't do them*, I'm not an idiot.

SOLOMON. You just, didn't do them? —

HOWIE. Dude, yes, of course, yes! *(Beat.)*

SOLOMON. People in Salem are pretty open-minded.

HOWIE. People in Salem are straight. I don't know, I'm new here, I grew up in Portland, but … people here think they're liberal, but most are like liberal Puritans. I can't even find a teacher to be the advisor for the Gay/Straight Alliance.

SOLOMON. Is that like — / What is — ?

HOWIE. It's not a big deal, I just need to find an advisor or else I don't get any school funding.

SOLOMON. *(Smiling.)* Well … have you asked the mayor? I bet he'd do it …

HOWIE. Right, our mayor who won't give me any civil rights, but *will* give me a blowjob …

SOLOMON. *(Laughing.)* That's disgusting …

HOWIE. *You're* disgusting, stop freaking out about stuff so much, you're like an old man —

SOLOMON. I'm not an old man, I'm not — why would you … I'm not an old man … and … *(Beat.)* I'm not an old man. But, I don't know, sometimes I think the best part of being young is knowing that there are all of these unhappy older people around who wish they were my age. *(Beat.)* Like, the good part isn't going to football games or house parties … it's just … the best part is being envied. Is that awful?

HOWIE. You're very serious …

SOLOMON. *You're* very serious … *(Beat.)*

HOWIE. You want to know the truth about Mr. Healy?

SOLOMON. Yes. *Yes. (Solomon adjusts the tape recorder.)*

HOWIE. I haven't told anyone this … *(Blackout.)*

Scene 5: Dramatic/Humorous Interpretation

A sign that reads, "Speech & Debate — be the 1st Team Members of North Salem's newest club!"

Diwata and Solomon are the only people in the room. Diwata stands in front. Solomon sits, observing. She lifts her head to signal the beginning of her introduction.

DIWATA. *(Speaking to an imaginary audience.)* In Salem, everything and everyone belongs to either God or the Devil; dissent is not merely unlawful, it is associated with satanic activity. As Danforth says in Act Three, "a person is either with this court or he must be counted against it." And so, in the following scene from Arthur Miller's classic *The Crucible*, I invite you to enter a world in which some girls are good and some girls are bitches who pretend to be witches, hot flow, yo ho, and so, get ready to know a girl named Mary Warren. Accused of witchcraft, Mary stands before the court unsure of whether or not telling the truth will set her free, or set her on fire. *(Solomon looks around to see if anyone else has entered. Or understands what Diwata is saying. Diwata checks an index card.)* The townsfolk became active in all of the madness not merely out of religious piety and goody goodness; but also because it allowed them to act out every dark desire and hateful urge under the cover of righteousness. The secrets the girls released were able to thrive only because other people benefited from them. What good is a secret, if people can keep it? *(Beat.)* With that in mind, get ready, because something wicked this way is coming, and if you feel flames, don't pull the fire alarm … it's just feeling hot because things are really heating up … in … *The Crucible*, by Arthur Miller. *(Diwata drops her head, preparing for her performance. With each of the following lines of dialogue, Diwata changes her focal point [and possibly her voice] to indicate that she is becoming "another character." Her attempt is earnest, not psychotic.)*

> *(As Danforth.)* You are charging Abigail Williams with a marvelous cool plot to murder, do you understand that?
> *(As Proctor.)* I do, sir. I believe she means to murder.
> *(As Danforth.)* This child would murder your wife?
> *(As Proctor.)* It is not a child, sir. It is a whore.

(Solomon raises his hand, interrupts.)

SOLOMON. I'm sorry, I have no idea what you're doing. What are you doing?

DIWATA. Please don't interrupt. Just experience my demonstration first, then I'll explain the rules, 'kay? *(Diwata drops her head in preparation for her performance. She raises her head and begins again.)*

> *(As Danforth.)* You are charging Abigail Williams with a marvelous cool plot to murder, do you understand that?
> *(As Proctor.)* I do, sir. I believe she means to murder.
> *(As Danforth.)* This child would murder your wife?
> *(As Proctor.)* It is not a child, sir. It is a whore.

(Solomon raises his hand, interrupts.)

SOLOMON. Okay, I'm not even following —

DIWATA. *(Sighs, upset.)* This category is called Dramatic Interpretation and I'm performing a scene from *The Crucible.* You perform all of the parts of the play yourself, that's what you do for this event.

SOLOMON. Why would you do that, perform all of the parts?

DIWATA. Because those are the rules of the National Forensics League. People in the know call this category "D.I.," which is the slang terminology for Dramatic Interpretation.

SOLOMON. What? I don't know what you're saying.

DIWATA. Speech & Debate has its own lingo. I'll teach you all the terms, don't worry.

SOLOMON. I'm not / worried …

DIWATA. Have you even read *The Crucible?* We did it in the fall, amazing play. I love big fat epic stuff. *Hamlet, Angels in America, Wicked —*

SOLOMON. You were in *The Crucible* here? I saw that. Who did you play?

DIWATA. I was an extra, I looked like a fat pilgrim, whatever. I didn't even have a name. I called myself Goody Goodyear.

SOLOMON. That's funny.

DIWATA. I didn't even get cast as Tituba. Healy said she was black, which — historically the character was Native Indian, or South American Arawak, some shit like that so … whatever, I can't believe I didn't get Tituba. Whatever.

SOLOMON. That sucks.

DIWATA. Yeah, but I went as Mary Warren for Halloween which was pretty sweet revenge. I dyed my waitress uniform black and — it looked fierce. I like, *was* Mary Warren. I ran around screaming, having breakdowns — it was amazing. What did you go as last year?

SOLOMON. I didn't go as anything. But wait — which one is Mary Warren?

DIWATA. She's the girl who basically knows that all the other girls are just pretending to be witches, but in the end, she realizes she'll hang if she doesn't lie … so she saves herself. She holds it in.

SOLOMON. She lies.

DIWATA. She holds the truth in.

SOLOMON. That's lame.

DIWATA. No, no, there's nothing brave about her telling the truth and then dying.

SOLOMON. Sure there is. That main guy, the lead, that's what he does. It's noble.

DIWATA. Yeah, and he goes to the gallows and leaves his pregnant wife behind. Real noble. He should have kept his mouth shut.

SOLOMON. You're just trying to sound all badass.

DIWATA. No I'm not — that one scene, where the old man in town, Giles Corey dies — they piled stones on him because he wouldn't admit to witchcraft. His last words were supposedly — and this is as they were piling stones on him — "more weight." My last words would have been: "Get these fucking stones off my chest."

SOLOMON. Whatever, I don't believe you'd do that. *(Beat.)* What?

DIWATA. Nothing. You look familiar.

SOLOMON. Sorry, do we know each other?

DIWATA. No. Don't worry about it, just seen you around. Those sneakers stand out. *(Beat.)* Anyway, you'll have to help me come up with a short demonstration of the different categories for the school board — you know, show them what Speech & Debate is, why they should support it. That's Miss Langan's only requirement. Well, that and we need at least three people to get some basic funding, and … to properly execute some of my original work … but, I'm sure — that other girl just left to go to the bathroom, I think.

SOLOMON. Twenty-five minutes ago.

DIWATA. She's taking a dump.

SOLOMON. I'm not here to join the team.

DIWATA. What?

SOLOMON. I'm writing an article for the paper and wanted to ask you a few questions. I was just waiting around for the meeting to finish …

DIWATA. Oh.

SOLOMON. Can we do a quick interview? If that girl comes back from the bathroom, we can stop …

DIWATA. Well … okay. Wow. Okay. But … you might want to join after I explain the other events — you'd like Extemporaneous Commentary, that's where a contestant draws three questions on a topic, selects one —

SOLOMON. — then has thirty minutes to prepare an answer to the question, I know — I researched the categories to see if I was interested … but I'm not.

DIWATA. What kind of research did you do?

SOLOMON. I googled Speech & Debate.

DIWATA. *(A bit threatened.)* Because the kids call that category "extemp comm," that's the lingo for that event. I don't know if you were able to get the lingo from your research. Your googling.

SOLOMON.	DIWATA.
Uh, no.	I'll teach it to you, don't worry.

I'm not worried.

DIWATA. Do you know about the debate categories as well, like cross-ex debate, which is the slang termination for Cross-Examination debate, did you hear that hot flow, yo —

SOLOMON. Yo ho, I know, I heard, you keep doing that. Look, Diwanda —

DIWATA. Di*wata*.

SOLOMON. — I'm not here to write about the Speech & Debate team.

DIWATA. Then what are you writing about? *(Beat.)*

SOLOMON. Do you know anything about Mr. Healy having any inappropriate relationships with students?

DIWATA. Whoa, why would you think I'd know something like that?

SOLOMON. You said some things on … I found a link to your podcast from your blog —

DIWATA. My blog? You read my blog?

SOLOMON. Calm down …

DIWATA. Why didn't you say something before?

SOLOMON. I didn't want to freak you out …

DIWATA. That's my private journal!

SOLOMON. Which you post daily on the World Wide Web!

DIWATA. If you aren't here to join the team I'm going to have to ask you to leave —

SOLOMON. What? Why?

DIWATA. … so I can conduct the rest of the meeting!

SOLOMON. I'm the only person who showed up!

DIWATA. *(Not allowing herself to cry.)* Please just leave, okay, *go* …

SOLOMON. I'm sorry …

DIWATA. *(Looking towards the door.)* That girl better be shitting … dammit … *(Solomon gets some papers out of his bag. He tentatively approaches Diwata.)*

SOLOMON. Can you look at this? I think you might talk to me if you read this.

DIWATA. What is it?

SOLOMON. Read it.

DIWATA. *(Examining the papers.)* This is a script?

SOLOMON. Just read this for me … *(Beat. Diwata collects herself.)*

DIWATA. *(Looking at the script.)* So, should I read both parts —
just perform it cold?
SOLOMON. I was thinking you'd just read it silently, but …
DIWATA. I'll look this way when I'm BiGuy and this way when
I'm BlondBoi okay?
SOLOMON. Uh … I — fine, you can if you want, but … fine.
*(Diwata takes her performance very seriously. She shifts her focus when
she switches from BiGuy to BlondBoi.)*
DIWATA.

> *(As BiGuy.)* how old are u?
> *(As BlBoi.)* just turned 18
> *(As BiGuy.)* im scared
> *(As BlBoi.)* y?
> *(As BiGuy.)* u r 2 young
> *(As BlBoi.)* says who?
> *(As BiGuy.)* the police

SOLOMON. Please, just — read the rest to yourself —
DIWATA. *(Reading ahead.)* Is this a new play? — it's kind of dirty —
SOLOMON. No, no, it's real. It's a real transcript from an online
chat.
DIWATA. Really?
SOLOMON. Mr. Healy is "BiGuy."
DIWATA. What?
SOLOMON. "BlondBoi" is a new student here, a transfer. Keep
reading …
DIWATA. *(Flipping through the transcript.)* Where did this come from?
SOLOMON. On your website — someone posted a message to
your bulletin board, this kid — "BlondBoi" posted a message and
his phone number for you … *(Takes out a sheet of paper.)* Here, I
printed it out …
DIWATA. I know, I saw it, but I don't respond to freaks who post
their numbers online …
SOLOMON. I did.
DIWATA. You *called* him?
SOLOMON. I'm a reporter — I wanted to find out the dirt he
had on Mr. Healy …
DIWATA. And this kid talked to you?
SOLOMON. Yeah, he said they were gonna meet up at Riverfront
Park, but then he recognized Healy's email address from his class
syllabus and got freaked out …

DIWATA. Riverfront Park? Oh my God I'm never going / there again …

SOLOMON. … so I was like, I said to him, "How do I know you're not making all this up" or whatever — and I got him to email me the transcript!

DIWATA. *(Looking at the transcript.)* So this is actually real?

SOLOMON. I'm a reporter, you need to get proof.

DIWATA. If this gets out …

SOLOMON. I know, I know …

DIWATA. … will he be … arrested, do you think, or …

SOLOMON. Well, Healy didn't think he was a student here — BlondBoi's profile still says he's from Portland, so …

DIWATA. I can't believe / this …

SOLOMON. … and in this instance the kid is eighteen, it wasn't really illegal, but if … if *you* know something too … it could help define this as a pattern as opposed to —

DIWATA. Sorry, can't help you …

SOLOMON. But — then why did you say that stuff on your blog?

DIWATA. I heard some rumors going around about Healy, nothing concrete.

SOLOMON. Well, what were the rumors? They might be relevant.

DIWATA. No, I started them.

SOLOMON. Oh. So —

DIWATA. Look, I've answered your questions, and I — I need to focus on Speech & Debate right now, there's a chance I might have latecomers —

SOLOMON. Why are you pretending to care about Speech & Debate — you're only doing it because you can't get a part in the school musical —

DIWATA. I got a part, you asshole! I could have done the show if I wanted.

SOLOMON. You got a part?

DIWATA. Featured ensemble. Which is — for starters, FYI, most kids just got plain old ensemble, number one …

SOLOMON. Then why aren't you doing it?

DIWATA. … because number two, let me finish, featured ensemble is unacceptable when you spend three weeks preparing your audition song. Completely unacceptable. Any other director would have given me the lead. If you saw my audition you would get it.

SOLOMON. I doubt that.

DIWATA. Screw you, you use cover-up to hide your acne and think people can't tell. *(Solomon gets his bookbag, goes to leave.)* Do you even *know* what I did for my audition, for *Once Upon a Mattress?*
SOLOMON. Huh? ... no —
DIWATA. The lead in *Once Upon a Mattress*, Winnefred, she sings this big song in Act Two that's kind of a mock-striptease number. So I sang the song ... and underneath all my clothes, I had on a nude bodystocking, so ... do you see where I'm going with this?
SOLOMON. No.
DIWATA. Well, there I am, belting my brains out and as the song progresses, I start removing bits of my clothing so by the time I finish, all my clothes are on the floor. And I'm wearing nothing but the bodystocking —
SOLOMON. Did it look like you were really nude?
DIWATA. No — I mean, I had no nipples or anything. Nudity wasn't the point.
SOLOMON. Why wouldn't Winnefred have nipples?
DIWATA. That's not the point. I shouldn't have told you. God.
SOLOMON. What was the point?
DIWATA. To take a risk, to get noticed. I'm not going to get cast for my golden hair, or tall frame, or cheekbones, I'm, I'm — I actually have pretty good cheekbones, but it's — I'm ready to be noticed. You can't understand, you're not in my profession.
SOLOMON. Well — no, but ... no, there was this kid who published a novel when he was twelve, which ... *(Beat.)* But then, some writers don't hit it big until they're old, in their thirties or forties even.
DIWATA. Yeah, well you'll never hit it big if you keep pursuing stories you can't get printed ...
SOLOMON. What does that mean?
DIWATA. Where are you going to publish the piece you're writing? I mean, the school paper won't let you write about a teacher in the building ...
SOLOMON. I know, my dad has this friend at the *Oregonian*, I'm thinking I can show it to her, they'd publish it there.
DIWATA. But ... I mean, you realize once you show it to her, she'll pass it off to a *real* journalist to write the *actual* story. I mean ... right?
SOLOMON. But — and I *am* a real journalist, first of all ...
DIWATA. You're a kid. Look at you, obviously, you have this weird agenda —

SOLOMON. Shutup, I don't have — I'm, obviously, yes, I want to get my foot in the door as a writer, but it's —

DIWATA. You're not going to get your foot in the door that way, trust me … but …

SOLOMON. What?

DIWATA. *(Subtly proceeding with her plan.)* … No, I'm just thinking, I could help you out if you wanted … I could, if you wanted, I could make your article part of my Speech & Debate presentation. I could have your words read in front of the entire school board if you helped me by joining / the team —

SOLOMON. No, thank you — I don't like performing …

DIWATA. All the meetings are broadcast live on public access TV.

SOLOMON. No one watches public access —

DIWATA. That's not the point, it'll be preserved on record, your reporting would be —

SOLOMON. No — I don't like performing …

DIWATA. There are lots of categories — we could use Original Oratory, *I* could read your article word for word as a speech, think of it as broadcast journalism —

SOLOMON. No, okay?

DIWATA. Can you imagine having all of these school board members behind a long table listening to us … wondering, "Who is this fierce talent? Why the hell wasn't *she* Laurey in last year's production of *Oklahoma*? That other girl they cast didn't even have a vibrato / and —"

SOLOMON. What are you talking / about — ?

DIWATA. … and saying, "*This* boy's writing is undeniably good. Where has *this* kid been hiding, why haven't *his* stories been running on the front of every issue of *The Trojan*?" —

SOLOMON. Well, because the school board thinks — it's *censorship*, three times they've — I wrote this amazing piece about … ugh … yeah, I mean, yes, I do like the idea of … I mean, this is a district that won't let me write about abortion or our own mayor's scandal in the school paper — so yeah, the thought of a forum in which they are *forced* to listen —

DIWATA. Good then just, just consider it …

SOLOMON. Wouldn't we … get in trouble if I —

DIWATA. For turning in a child molester? I mean, that's what you think he is, right? Based on your talk with this kid? *(Beat.)*

SOLOMON. Lemme think about it.

DIWATA. Think about it, yeah ... I'm just ... I'm glad you came today. We do need to find one more person to get fundraising and some rehearsal space, you know, but ... I can do that unless you have a friend who wants —

SOLOMON. Most of my friends are at other schools or from youth group, you know?

DIWATA. Oh sure, sure. Mine are mostly older, they've graduated, so ...

SOLOMON. *(Getting out his bookbag.)* Here, let me give you my number ... *(Solomon has to remove a his iPhone to reach a business card in the bottom of his bag. Diwata picks it up, looks at the screen.)*

DIWATA. You're listening to George Michael? On repeat?

SOLOMON. Oh, yeah, that's — nothing, just wanted to hear a song ... *(Solomon takes his iPhone back.)*

DIWATA. You know George Michael was arrested for masturbating in a public bathroom, something like that, right?

SOLOMON. What?

DIWATA. Is that why you like him?

SOLOMON. No. That's disgusting. Why would you say that?

DIWATA. Because I think that's how people remember him.

SOLOMON. I don't know, I think it's disgusting. I'll see you later, my dad's probably waiting outside for me. *(Solomon exits. Diwata spies the piece of paper Solomon left behind, the printout of Howie's post. She picks it up, thinks. She checks to see that he is gone, picks up her phone and dials.)*

DIWATA. *(On the phone.)* Hi, is this — this is the girl who wrote the "monoblog" — you posted your number for me? *(Looking outside the door.)* ... we should talk ... *(Blackout.)*

Scene 6: Cross-Ex

Howie sits at a table in a restaurant. Diwata stands next to him, wearing her waitress uniform, coffee pot in hand. The uniform is unflattering — a one-piece "dress" (which goes down to her calves), complete with a white apron in front. Howie is uneasy.

DIWATA. ... Sometimes, when all the stalls are taken in the girls' room at school, I use the boys' bathroom on the third floor, because no one is ever up there after three. And I shout first, I say, "Anyone in there?" You know, something like that ...

HOWIE. Can't you sit down? I feel really weird sitting here by myself ...

DIWATA. I can't take a break for another ten minutes ... and I have an appointment this afternoon —

HOWIE. Just keep going ...

DIWATA. So last year when we were rehearsing for *The Crucible*, there was a line of girls, we were all in costume waiting to use the bathroom ... so I went up to the third floor, and I yelled into the boys' room. No one answered, so I went in. I finished going to the bathroom, and I heard footsteps. Normally, I'd rattle around, make noise pulling toilet paper out, you know, trying to let someone know I'm there, I'm a master at masking the sound of plopping poop. *(Howie is not amused.)* But because this is the guys' bathroom ... I just kind of hold my breath, thinking I'll wait it out. *(Beat.)* And then more footsteps. Maybe they came in together, I can't remember ... but I could see them through the crack in the side of the door. Mr. Healy for sure, and then him, with those white sneakers. Their backs were to me.

HOWIE. And you're sure it was him?

DIWATA. Positive. He never looked at Mr. Healy, both of them seemed to be peeing, but then Solomon seemed to be standing further away from the urinal, like he was ... I dunno ... like he was trying to show Mr. Healy his ... you know? *(Beat.)* And there was some touching, I don't remember exactly how it started, because then I breathed, I inhaled, they must have heard; they didn't check to see who was in the stall, they just bolted, both of them. And that was it. I sat in there for about twenty minutes. I was scared. *I* was scared, isn't that weird? *(Beat.)* Anyway, I brought the Speech & Debate rule book … *(Puts the Speech & Debate rule book on the table.)* I know you only agreed to do one category, but you should consider double-entering. That's the lingo kids use when they do two events, double-entering.

HOWIE. Do you think it's because he's religious? All that Catholic guilty stuff, is that what it is? —

DIWATA. Hey I'm Catholic, that's not it.

HOWIE. You're not practicing, are you?

DIWATA. Just relax, okay? And you should really order something …

HOWIE. No. Solomon's getting jerked off by a teacher after school and he wants to go public with what he knows about *me*? Is he insane? Little closeted faggot …

DIWATA. He can't say anything about you. If he wants to talk about you, we talk about him.

HOWIE. You could have told me this over the phone.

DIWATA. Don't get pissy with me, I'm doing you a favor. I didn't have to tell you any of this. I told you because —

HOWIE. I'm not joining the Speech & Debate team —

DIWATA. *You promised* —

HOWIE. Please *sit down*. We don't even know each other, this is so weird —

DIWATA. You *promised*, and FYI, it's not weird for me to spend time talking at tables, most customers love me, just FYI —

HOWIE. Why didn't you say something?

DIWATA. When?

HOWIE. Last year, when you saw all that?

DIWATA. What would I have said? — Mom, today I saw a teacher and a student touching each other in their bathing suit areas?

HOWIE. Bathing — / what?

DIWATA. It's from stranger-danger, you don't remember that? …

HOWIE. No, I was in a different / school …

DIWATA. I mean, I guess it's better than someone telling me, "Strangers shouldn't touch your *vagina*," but still —

HOWIE. Okay, be quiet, people are staring.

DIWATA. Obviously you don't want this to get out …

HOWIE. If Solomon opens his mouth and I'm known as the

pervert cruising for online sex, you think I'm going to get a Gay/ Straight Alliance started?

DIWATA. People have their own secrets.

HOWIE. People care. That's why being in Salem is so ... *(Beat.)* I hate that straight fraternity dudes can have their porn and Howard Stern can talk about doing women up the ass ... and they're just normal straight guys — but if there was a *gay* Howard Stern on the air —

DIWATA. I like Howard Stern.

HOWIE. That's not what I'm saying ...

DIWATA. What does this have to do with Solomon? You're out, you're proud, you can do whatever you want. Probably more things than other minorities. More than women. / Stop whining.

HOWIE. No way, no way ...

DIWATA. Oh, yes, *yes* ... homophobia is so 1985. Most people think it's cool.

HOWIE. It's not "cool" ... it's not *trendy* ... it's *biology* ...

DIWATA. Shhh ... I'm just saying — *(Noticing her manager.)* — spill your coffee or something, help me look busy ...

HOWIE. What?

DIWATA. Do it! *(Howie knocks over his coffee. Diwata pulls out a rag from her apron, sits down and begins to wipe up the table.)*

HOWIE. Jesus Christ ...

DIWATA. People our age *don't even have these hang-ups*, by the time we're adults *these won't even be* issues ... *(Finishing cleaning up.)* ... and I didn't mean for you to spill the whole cup. Dammit ... *(Beat.)*

HOWIE. Would people really think awful things about me if they saw that chat transcript?

DIWATA. I'm a double minority ...

HOWIE. What, you're — what are you talking about?

DIWATA. If you want to whine about being gay, I'm just / saying ...

HOWIE. I wasn't whining ...

DIWATA. ... I'm female and Filipino.

HOWIE. You don't look Filipino.

DIWATA. You don't look gay. *(She smiles.)* Yes you do.

HOWIE. It's the hair, right? Is it the hair?

DIWATA. Yes, BlondBoi. And P.S. — what shade of blond are you — *ebony*?

HOWIE. Shutup, the name gets guys' attention — and, I bleached my hair last summer, so —

DIWATA. My grandmother was half-Filipino. I'm an eighth. My kids someday will be … a sixteenth? Is that how that works, you just keep dividing?

HOWIE. I guess. And what do you mean "someday," from your podcast, it seems like you're …

DIWATA. That I'm what?

HOWIE. … expecting? Or …

DIWATA. Expecting what?

HOWIE. Aren't you…? *(Howie rubs his stomach.)*

DIWATA. Hungry?

HOWIE. Diwata …

DIWATA. I'm not pregnant.

HOWIE. I thought in your podcast / you said —

DIWATA. I'm not pregnant. I was drunk, if I said —

HOWIE. Really?

DIWATA. Yeah …

HOWIE. 'Cause I work at Januzzi's, that pizza / place near —

DIWATA. Yeah, I know where it is —

HOWIE. — near the family planning center. *(Beat.)* I saw you go in there last week.

DIWATA. No, it wasn't me —

HOWIE. You had your uniform on, which … is kind of memorable. *(Beat.)* Anyway … *(Trying to lighten the tension.)* … how classic is it that in a Salem strip mall you can get an abortion and a slice of pepperoni pizza in one shot, you know? *(Beat.)* Sorry, I didn't … I'm sorry if it's a secret or something.

DIWATA. Yeah, it is, and I was there for my friend, FYI. I wanted to be there for her.

HOWIE. Oh …

DIWATA. Yeah, I can see how you would think that, though —

HOWIE. Yeah, especially 'cause you went in by yourself.

DIWATA. Yeah, I was late. *(Fighting back tears.)* All right sir, I'll be right back with some fries.

HOWIE. What? *(Diwata exits, reenters with a plate of fries. She sits down.)* I shouldn't have said anything, I'm sorry …

DIWATA. I'm going back today. To that center. For — obviously … but … have you told lots of kids? Who knows?

HOWIE. Who would I tell, I don't know anyone here. I just want to get my senior year over with, what do I care what you do? I could care less. *(Howie eats a fry.)* These are terrible.

DIWATA. They're left over from that lady's table. *(Howie spits the fry into a napkin.)*

HOWIE. I hate Salem …

DIWATA. Have you ever had a scare like this? With a girlfriend, or …

HOWIE. Uh, no. But I've never had sex with a woman.

DIWATA. Never?

HOWIE. I came out real young, when I was ten.

DIWATA. Was your first time … was it —

HOWIE. Uh, it was fine.

DIWATA. Yeah?

HOWIE. Yeah. *(Beat.)*

DIWATA. Were you *ten*?

HOWIE. No, no, I was not ten.

DIWATA. Mine was fine, but a mess, you know how it is. It didn't even go all the way in. I'm not sure it even counts, I don't know how that works. No one tells you that.

HOWIE. Does your mom know, or —

DIWATA. If my mom knew I'd be going to hell and sitting through a lecture on the rhythm method.

HOWIE. Where are your friends?

DIWATA. They're older, most of them graduated.

HOWIE. Where's the father?

DIWATA. The day after we did it, I called just to say "hey" or whatever, and he was like, "I never would have slept with you if I wasn't so drunk." So … *(Beat.)*

HOWIE. So you guys are getting married?

DIWATA. *(Smiling.)* Yeah. We're getting married in the spring. *(Beat.)*

HOWIE. So … what are we going to say to Solomon?

DIWATA. Nothing. If you tell him, the Speech & Debate team will fall apart —

HOWIE. I don't care about the — I care about my reputation.

DIWATA. I care about mine. I need this, I *need* some form of performance this year that's school-sanctioned, something official for my transcript. How am I supposed to make it as an actress if I can't even find work in my own school district? I need three people to do this presentation, and you promised you'd join the team if I told you …

HOWIE. No, not if he wants to use my chat transcript as material!

42

DIWATA. *I'll* be the one reading it out loud.

HOWIE. Yeah so —

DIWATA. I won't actually do it. Right before our presentation I'll tell him I want to switch pieces — Solomon's too nervous to present any of his stuff himself.

HOWIE. What if he isn't —

DIWATA. Then, then, we out him. *(Beat.)* You're gonna help me. I didn't have to tell you any of this.

HOWIE. If he pisses me off, I'm gonna say something …

DIWATA. Then I tell people what I know about you, *BlondBoi* …

HOWIE. That I — what, that I'm messing around online, looking for — / go ahead …

DIWATA. Looking to have sex with older guys, yeah, well good, then, you won't be embarrassed if people find out …

HOWIE. I'm gonna go …

DIWATA. Okay. *(Howie doesn't move. Beat.)* Did you leave yet? *(Howie throws a fry at Diwata. Beat.)* The fries aren't from anyone's table, that was a lie.

HOWIE. *(Taking a fry.)* I don't believe you but I'm starving.

DIWATA. Distract me. My appointment's in an hour. Tell me a story.

HOWIE. I can't think of any. *(He sees Diwata is anxious. Diwata puts her head down on the table. Beat. Howie sighs, he can't believe he's actually going to do this …)* Once upon a time, there was this kid who always wanted to time travel. And one day he got his wish and went all the way back to Biblical times … *(Howie continues the story as the lights fade to black and music fades in …)*

Scene 7: Duo Interpretation

… The mysterious musical vamp continues, coming from Diwata's Casio keyboard.

Weary from time travel, Mary Warren, played by Diwata, enters looking more like a fat pilgrim. While it has many new frills, Diwata's waitress uniform (dyed black) forms the base of her Mary Warren costume.

Mary Warren notices Teenage Abraham Lincoln, played by Howie. He has a thin beard and perhaps a top hat.

DIWATA. *(As Mary Warren.)* Where am I? I must have fallen through a worm hole and travelled back in time. But to when? And to where? *(Seeing Teenage Abraham Lincoln.)*
  Boy, whatcha doin'?
  Boy, whatcha thinkin'?
  Boy, what's your name?
HOWIE. *(As Teenage Abraham Lincoln.)*
  It's Abraham Lincoln
DIWATA.
  I've landed in a land
  That's strange and foreign
HOWIE.
  Girl, tell me your name
DIWATA.
  It's Mary Warren
  Boy, I'm from Salem
  I just had my trial
  They think I'm a witch
  They think I'm vile
  They said girl you'll hang, you must confess
  So I lied and said, yes — I am possessed
HOWIE.
  You held it in?

DIWATA.
I held it in
HOWIE.
But Mary, you lied
DIWATA.
I held it in
HOWIE.
Don't you feel awful?
DIWATA.
Yes, but I'm alive
(An aside to the audience.)
This girl is headstrong
(Back to Abe.)
Abe, I lied in court
But what the heck
I lost my honor
Not my neck

(The following interlude occurs over the musical vamp. Howie might have to reference a sheet of paper for the dialogue. He is wooden, uncomfortable with the text. Solomon watches in morbid fascination off to the side.)

HOWIE. Wow, Mary. This makes me think twice about a talk I was going to have with my parents today.

DIWATA. What kind of talk, Abraham?

HOWIE. *(Wooden.)* Oh, you know. Just, I wanted to share with them that I'm a little different. That I love them, but I also love the way the army men look in and out of their uniforms, that kind of stuff.

DIWATA. You want my advice, Abraham?

HOWIE. Yes, Mary Warren. *(She resumes the song, in full belt.)*

DIWATA.
Hold it in
HOWIE.
I shouldn't tell them?
DIWATA.
Not on your life
Hold it in

HOWIE.
But they'll still love me
DIWATA.
Boy, get a wife
(An aside to the audience.)
A sexy lady.
(Back to Abe.)
Don't you want to run the country someday?
HOWIE.
Yes — you think I can do it?
DIWATA.
Not if you're gay
HOWIE.
But I'm bright, I'm moral
I could win
DIWATA.
Trust me, I'm a Puritan
HOWIE.
I'll hold it in
DIWATA.
Just hold it in
Keep your feelings inside
Hold it in
HOWIE. *(Riffing.)*
Girl, I can't lie …
DIWATA.
Boy, swallow your pride
(Upset, breaking character, to Howie.) Please don't riff …
HOWIE.
If I hold it in
I lose my bravery
DIWATA.
If you hold it in
You will end slavery
You win
HOWIE.
I win
DIWATA and HOWIE.
If you (I) hold it in.
(Beat. Teenage Abe and Mary Warren hold hands. Diwata nods to

Solomon, indicating that this is his cue. Solomon addresses the audience, reading from an index card. The musical vamp continues in the background. Diwata has every line of Solomon's speech [which she wrote] memorized. Occasionally, she unintentionally mouths the words.)

SOLOMON. Two teenagers … lost … separated by different times, yet united in their quest to speak their minds. Far-fetched? Perhaps. But far from true? — far from it. *(Solomon doesn't understand what he just read. He looks to Diwata. She urges him to continue while trying not to break her character/pose. Solomon rolls his eyes, continues.)* Teenagers today are holding lots of things inside. Feelings, fears, and guns. *(Mary Warren hikes up her skirt to reveal a gun attached to her leg. Reading:)* But by keeping things hidden inside, who are kids really helping? Themselves? Or the adults who would rather ignore uncomfortable subjects rather than engage them? After all, do we live in Salem, Oregon, or Salem, Massachusetts circa 16-insert-the-date-of-whenever-the-witches-were-burned? *(Solomon, perplexed, turns to Diwata who stares daggers at him, once again urging him to continue. Frustrated, he continues:)* Puritanism seems to be lingering in our country. So I ask: Would Mary Warren's naked forest-dancing be any more welcome today? Let's find out. *(Beat.)* At this point, Solomon, Diwata and Howie strip down to nude bodystockings and do some naked forest-dancing — *(To Diwata.)* Okay, I'm sorry, no way, no way — *(Solomon tears the index card up.)*

HOWIE. A nude bodystocking? You're retarded, Diwata. *(Diwata turns the music off.)*

DIWATA. It will be tasteful if you guys can commit. Trust me.

HOWIE. What's a nude bodystocking?

DIWATA. I can show you mine —

SOLOMON. No, stop. *Stop.* I agreed to participate, but there will be no naked forest-dancing in the presentation. This is from your musical, isn't it?

DIWATA. It also falls within the rules of Group Interpretation — *(Reading from the rulebook.)* — "Group Interpretation is just that — the group interpretation of a narrative, also known as Readers' Theatre. Material may be original. Costumes, props, visual aids … prohibited." Shit, so we lose the costumes …

SOLOMON. The costumes aren't the problem. It's the material.

DIWATA. When Howie told me the stories you guys wrote as kids, I realized that they were the missing link to the story *I've* been trying to write. Mary Warren *time travels* …

SOLOMON. Oh my God …

DIWATA. … she meets various figures in American history: Abe Lincoln, Martin Luther King, Jr., Idina Menzel —

SOLOMON. I never gave you permission to use my story —

DIWATA. You can't trademark Teenage Abraham Lincoln, and as Team Captain …

SOLOMON. Self-appointed / Team Captain …

DIWATA. … I think it's important for the school board to see us working together for at least one category. And Group Interpretation is a way for us to do that, to tell a story together.

SOLOMON. Then we do it, but we come up with material that we each have a hand in creating.

HOWIE. Can we please get this over with? Please.

DIWATA. Fine. We will do Group Interpretation together, material TBD for the category AKA G.I. sans Joe, you know, hot flow —

SOLOMON. Yo ho, I know.   HOWIE. Yo ho, yo ho, I know. Moving on …

DIWATA. Moving on … as Team Captain —

SOLOMON. *Self-appointed* Team / Captain …

DIWATA. — I would like to — I'm not acknowledging those remarks — I would like to do a check-in with all of the members of the team and get a progress report. Can we all get in a circle? Please? Thanks. *(Howie and Solomon look at each other, sigh, and stand together to form a circle.)*

SOLOMON. This is a triangle.

DIWATA. *(Ignoring Solomon.)* Howie, can we have an update? You agreed to cover the category of Declamation.

HOWIE. Right. Well, I'll find a speech, no problem. That's it. Please move on. Please.

DIWATA. And Solomon?

SOLOMON. Well, Diwata was helping me do Original Oratory —

DIWATA. Double-O, yes …

SOLOMON. My plan was to have you read the article I wrote about, you know — the mayor and Mr. Healy and —

HOWIE. I can't wait to read that.

SOLOMON. Are you being sarcastic? —

DIWATA. He's being difficult. Howie's just nervous about how he will come off in all of this —

SOLOMON. No, don't worry … that's why … I'd like to have

some other material precede the speech … I'd like to use Howie's transcript.

DIWATA. I don't understand — you want me to read BiGuy and BlondBoi's chat first? —

SOLOMON. No, I want to showcase it myself using a different category — Poetry Reading.

HOWIE. How?

SOLOMON. I think it needs to be visual. I'm a wizard with PowerPoint, I could project the chat, and suddenly it's in its original form — it becomes physical, it's cyber-poetry, more importantly, it's indisputable … it's closer to real reporting, it's evidence …

HOWIE. This isn't a trial.

DIWATA. Yeah, and as proud as I am that you've learned about a new category, especially since Howie has never shown that kind of speech spirit, the rules say you're not allowed to use audio-visual.

SOLOMON. So we break the rules, the material itself will cause enough controversy, right?

HOWIE. I don't know …

SOLOMON. And we can have some music underscoring it — something ordinary to show that you're just some common kid — an ordinary boy who found himself in extraordinary circumstances. *(To Howie.)* So no one will think you're a freak.

HOWIE. Speak for yourself.

SOLOMON. What? What's that supposed to mean?

HOWIE. You keep looking at me all weird, like you hate me, like —

SOLOMON. What? You obviously have those feelings, / not me —

DIWATA. Okay, time out.

HOWIE. You're so … you're obsessed with being normal, you're so …

DIWATA. Let's move on, please …

SOLOMON. I'm so what? Tell me. What / am I?

HOWIE. All of your shirts have *alligators* on them, you're — it's like you're always in costume —

SOLOMON. I like my shirts, they —

HOWIE. You don't even have a personality, / you're so …

SOLOMON. — and it's a *crocodile*, it's a *crocodile*, so …

HOWIE. I hate the way you act, it makes me sick. *(Beat.)*

DIWATA. *(As if nothing harsh has been said, calmly contributing to the conversation.)* I hate when people use too much vibrato. When they're belting. *(She turns to Solomon.)* Your turn.

SOLOMON. *(To Diwata.)* You're not funny. *(Howie is pissed.*

Awkward silence.)

DIWATA. Okay ... now that that's settled ... next order of business is ... and, I'm not sure if I already told you guys already, but ... yeah, so I called that reporter Solomon's dad knows — the one from the *Oregonian*, and ...

SOLOMON. Diwata, why would you —

DIWATA. ... I'm talking, thanks, and she wants to come and meet with us before our presentation — do some sort of human-interest story on the formation of our Speech & Debate team. It's not a big deal —

SOLOMON. She's *my* contact — HOWIE. No way, we're not you shouldn't have called her   having some reporter talk to us. without telling me first —

DIWATA. It would just be about — I'd perform, you'd smile for ten minutes, it's good publicity for us —

SOLOMON. You're not performing, she's *my* contact — if she comes we're going to discuss *my* work, maybe I even — I'd have to break my story, to tell her about Healy ...

HOWIE. What? No way —

DIWATA. No — she'll steal the story and write it herself, we still save that for the presentation ...

SOLOMON. I know but I've been, I keep thinking maybe people should know now — like it's our responsibility to tell people ...

HOWIE. You're gonna regret it if you break this story —

SOLOMON. What's that supposed to mean?

DIWATA. He means — Mr. Healy will get fired ...

SOLOMON. *(To Diwata.)* Isn't that what you want? You're the one who's been talking about revenge.

HOWIE. But what has he done? I'm legal in the state of Oregon, so what's the big deal? Have you even ever *had* sex?

SOLOMON. Oh, well, now you're going off on a tangent ...

HOWIE. I'm just trying to understand why you're obsessed with stories of sexual misconduct. You started with the mayor, then when you learned about me and / Mr. Healy —

SOLOMON. I'm not obsessed, and they're related, so, like any good reporter, I pursued the story —

HOWIE. Is it newsworthy?

SOLOMON. Yes, the mayor's personal life is fair game because it conflicts with his public policy.

HOWIE. So that's the mayor, Mr. Healy isn't —

SOLOMON. I think his online behavior conflicts with what people in this town expect from a public school teacher, Howie. Do you disagree with that? How can you disagree with that?

DIWATA. All right, calm down ladies —

HOWIE. He didn't know I lived in Salem and — you're right, fine, yes — the whole thing is — I'm embarrassed about it okay? But it's private. Just because you know about it doesn't make you entitled to broadcast it.

SOLOMON. I disagree. What if he hurts another student?

HOWIE. Who did he hurt? *(Solomon walks away.)* *Who did he hurt!?*

SOLOMON. Stop yelling at me, I don't know!

DIWATA. Solomon, return to the circle please.

HOWIE. We're not meeting with her —

SOLOMON. It's not your decision.

HOWIE. Of course it is, I'm the one who will look like a freak!

SOLOMON. You should have thought about that before you had that chat. *(Beat.)* My dad's waiting for me outside, I gotta go. *(Solomon exits. Blackout.)*

Scene 8: Declamation

Howie stands at the front of the room, reading from a newspaper. Solomon and Diwata watch. Howie directs his speech at Solomon.

HOWIE. *(Reading.)* "As mayor of Salem, I want to sincerely apologize to you for the shame I have brought to the city and to my office. This week the *Statesman Journal* reported that I have visited a gay chat-line on the internet and had relationships with adult men. I don't deny that."

SOLOMON. What are you reading? — Is this supposed to be your speech? —

HOWIE. Why don't you let me finish. *(Continuing.)* "I have always considered a person's private life private and have respected others in this way. I intended to keep my private life private as well. And I apologize. I do ask one thing if you are willing. Since my cancer I've taken to prayer and believe it has healing power. Please pray for me."

DIWATA. *(To Solomon.)* That's from today's paper.

HOWIE. The mayor sent this in an email to all city employees.

SOLOMON. Declamation is usually the reading of a speech that's acclaimed, like, the Gettysburg Address or something. Not a public statement that has no literary or historical value.

HOWIE. At least he was man enough to apologize.

SOLOMON. Is that an apology?

HOWIE. That's why it's so sad, I mean, the man's already dead. His career's probably over and even then, he can barely bring himself to tell the truth — even when he's backed into a corner. It's awful.

SOLOMON. It's awful that he would bring up his cancer. I mean, where was his cancer while he was cruising the web for barely-articulate eighteen-year-old boys? And the part about adult relationships, that's a lie — just because the kids were legal he's calling them adult relationships.

HOWIE. Don't you think a lot of successful, powerful straight guys would spend time with teenage girls if they had the chance, if the girls were willing?

SOLOMON. No, I don't know, not if they were good people, and what's with your euphemisms — "spend time with teenage girls," that's a bit glossy, don't you think? You're not even capable of saying what you really mean.

HOWIE. Are you gay? *(Diwata looks away.)* Are you? *(Awful silence. Throughout the following exchange, Solomon does not lose his cool or indicate anything is wrong.)*

SOLOMON. What is this? Who are you talking to?

DIWATA. Solomon, we don't really care, it's just — if you are —

SOLOMON. What? *(Beat.)* If I am it's none of your business. What is this? *(Beat.)* It's none of your business.

HOWIE. According to you it is. It conflicts with your public —

SOLOMON. That's politics, that's — I have no — I'm not in politics, what is this, if you don't talk to me I'm leaving, what is this?

HOWIE. It's hypocritical if you're —

SOLOMON. And hypocrisy, *if* I was hypocritical, it would be irrelevant —

HOWIE. So you are hypocritical, then? What does that mean?

SOLOMON. What do you want me to say?

HOWIE. I want to know if you're gay.

SOLOMON. Why? What, is this because today I changed the style of my shirt? Huh? *(Trying to lighten the tension.)* I told you this would happen — I took your advice, dressed a little different and look, you're already assuming I'm gay. C'mon, guys, what is this? *(Beat.)*

DIWATA. It was me in the third floor bathroom last year — I saw you and Mr. Healy, I was the one in the stall. *(Solomon looks to both of them for an explanation.)*

HOWIE. If you use anything you know about us without our permission, we will tell people what we know about you. I'd like all the copies of our conversation back too, the transcripts you have. *(Beat.)*

SOLOMON. What did she tell you? Because — I don't even know what — what is this all about?

HOWIE. Solomon …

SOLOMON. No, I'm just saying I don't even know what you're talking about. *(Diwata and Howie aren't sure how to proceed.)*

DIWATA. Solomon, it's not a big deal …

SOLOMON. What did you see?

DIWATA. We're not going to tell anyone. Howie, tell him. We won't tell anyone.

SOLOMON. Oh, okay. Whatever. Sure. I don't even know what this is about.

DIWATA. I saw you.

SOLOMON. Whatever. I've got to go. *(Solomon starts to cough. He goes to the wastebasket. He throws up.)*

DIWATA. Oh my God … *(Solomon keeps coughing, throws up again.)*

HOWIE. *(To Diwata, unsure of what else to say or do.)* Are there any paper towels in here, or … *(Diwata gets some tissues. Howie is frozen. Solomon sits by the garbage can, not looking at them. Beat.)*

DIWATA. *(Still keeping her distance from Solomon.)* No one knows, I just told Howie … *(Solomon can't look at either of them. He buries his head, faces away. Diwata and Howie are unsure of what to do.)*

SOLOMON. *(Angrily.)* Do I have to say something to you? *(Howie and Diwata attempt to say something once or twice but stop. The whole experience is tense, awful, and quiet. A very, very long beat. Diwata looks to Howie, then cautiously approaches Solomon, unsure.)*

DIWATA. I lost my virginity with my sweatshirt on.

HOWIE. What?

DIWATA. *(To Howie.)* I feel bad, he looks like he's gonna kill himself, so I'm just saying … *(To Solomon.)* No one knows that, I never told anyone that.

HOWIE. Jesus Christ … leave him alone.

DIWATA. *(To Solomon.)* I was home, a little drunk on my mom's bed, and …

HOWIE. Oh my God …

DIWATA. … when it started, and I don't even remember how it all started, but it was happening and my pants were around my ankles …

HOWIE. Oh my God …

DIWATA. … wearing this lame sweatshirt I didn't even like, it was a hand-me-down from my cousin, I had to throw it away, I couldn't look at it after it was over. My mom found it in the garbage, and she was like — "Diwata, we need to give this to Goodwill if you're not going to wear it. You know we don't throw clothes out." *(Beat.)* I could have at least had a nice one on. I have a Champion sweatshirt I like, something nicer. *(Beat. To Solomon:)* I won't tell anyone. I promise. *(Beat. To Howie:)* Your turn.

HOWIE. Oh my God.

DIWATA. Do it. *(Beat.)*

HOWIE. I'm in love with Diwata.

DIWATA. How much do I hate you. I hate you so much. *(Diwata smacks Howie. Beat.)*

HOWIE. *(To Solomon — sincere, but not sentimental. Howie doesn't feel sorry for himself.)* That dance I made up, for the Boy Scouts talent show — I said I left before I could embarrass myself. Well, I *did* teach them the dance. And all the kids — guys younger than me laughed. The leaders all laughed, and — they did this thing where they tried to hide the fact that they were laughing — they were like shifting their weight, looking away so I couldn't see them smiling when — I could tell, obviously. And then they said we didn't have time to learn all of it, when — there was at least fifteen minutes left. It was really bad. The kids called me "Miss Gay B.S.A." So … *(Beat.)*

DIWATA. B.S.A. — bathing suit areas?

HOWIE. No, retard. Boy Scouts of America.

DIWATA. *(Teasing.)* You know, Mary Warren got in trouble for dancing naked in the forest with Tituba. It's nothing to be ashamed of.

HOWIE. You are so retarded, Diwata.

DIWATA. You are totally teaching me your moves.

HOWIE. Jesus Christ …

DIWATA. … And oh my God, I'm getting some killer ideas for our Group Interpretation performance. Do you guys want to hear them?

SOLOMON. No, of course not …   HOWIE. No, not now …

DIWATA. When?

HOWIE. *(Gesturing towards Solomon, who still has his head buried in his hands by the garbage can.)* Diwata …

DIWATA. *Howard*, no — my team, my chance to perform has taken a consistent back seat to all of your homo-drama, so let's just be clear. You're both doing this. You're not walking away from this team. Promise …

HOWIE. Diwata …

DIWATA. And I decide the material we perform for Group Interpretation. No crapping all over my ideas like you did last time, otherwise we'll never agree. Promise. *Promise.*

SOLOMON. No, I'm not doing it — not unless you promise that none of this leaves this room.

HOWIE. Whatever you want. One presentation, one performance, then we're done.

DIWATA. I'm really moved by our team spirit.

HOWIE. What is that smell?

SOLOMON. My vomit.

DIWATA. So nasty ...

HOWIE. *(To Solomon.)* Are you going to come out to your parents?

SOLOMON. Stop it, Howie. You think you know me. They already know, did you know that? No, so ...

HOWIE. Huh?

SOLOMON. I know you guys think you're some sort of private eyes, breaking the story ...

HOWIE. Well you never said you were gay.

SOLOMON. ... last summer my parents found me this camp ...

DIWATA. They know? Your parents know?

SOLOMON. ... which, for the first time addressed those gay issues ...

DIWATA. Like musical theater camp?

SOLOMON. No ...

HOWIE. What issues? You're gay, who cares? It's not an issue.

SOLOMON. Exodus — it's this camp for kids who are, what some people call us is "ex-gays," but —

HOWIE. Jesus ...

DIWATA. Let him talk ...

SOLOMON. Kids who are gay, but want to live a life free of ... kids who don't want to live the gay lifestyle. Who don't want to be promiscuous and stuff ...

HOWIE. Gay people don't have to be promiscuous, I can't believe you'd say that!

SOLOMON. Stop yelling at me —

HOWIE. She's *deranged*, that doesn't mean all *straight* people are.

DIWATA. Excuse me, *BlondBoi*?

SOLOMON. She doesn't go around sleeping with people she meets online.

DIWATA. I'm right here ...

HOWIE. I don't do that, Solomon!

DIWATA. Then why are you surfing for sex all the time —

HOWIE. Why did you get drunk at a party, get knocked up and spend an afternoon at an abortion clinic —

DIWATA. Howie!

SOLOMON. I *knew* you were pregnant!

DIWATA. *(To Howie.)* How could you say that?

HOWIE. I'm sorry —

SOLOMON. You had an abortion?

DIWATA. *(To Howie.)* Shut your mouth about it, you shut your mouth.

SOLOMON. I can't beli —

DIWATA. Shutup! *(Beat. The three of them aren't sure what to do.)*

HOWIE. So I guess … what happens now?

DIWATA. I don't know. Let's … I don't know …

SOLOMON. What you saw in the bathroom … it wasn't what you think …

DIWATA. Okay, but I saw … then, okay, *you* tell me, what happened?

SOLOMON. It wasn't — I wasn't hurt or anything …

HOWIE. But … okay, so …

SOLOMON. I don't know if … maybe, I think, you'll laugh …

HOWIE. I won't laugh …

SOLOMON. … but as a guy, I don't know if … maybe I lost my, you know, virginity … I don't know … *(Diwata smiles. Howie laughs quietly.)*

DIWATA. Uh, okay, I would have seen that. Trust me.

HOWIE. *(Trying not to laugh.)* No, it's not your virginity, bud, I doubt he went that far.

SOLOMON. Not in the bathroom. *(Howie and Diwata are caught off-guard.)* No, no, no — he didn't hurt me — *(Knocking at the door.)*

HOWIE. Solomon, if he —

SOLOMON. Really. He didn't hurt me, never … *(More knocking.)*

VOICE. *(Shouting, from outside.)* Hello…? Can I come in?

SOLOMON. This doesn't leave this room, okay? This doesn't leave this room … *(The Reporter enters.)*

REPORTER. Hello … oh, hi, guys. I'm sorry, sorry to interrupt. Hi. I'm Jan Clark, from the *Oregonian*. I'm sorry to interrupt. Hi, Solomon. Can I just sit down and observe? *(Long beat. Solomon, Diwata, and Howie look at each other, unsure of what to say. They are a collective mess.)* A friend of yours, a … Diwanda, we spoke last week. She's been leaving me voicemails asking if I'd stop by one of your rehearsals and … your dad, Solomon, he mentioned you were here rehearsing, so … *(Beat.)* He said he'd call you on your cell to tell you I was coming.

SOLOMON. My cell was turned off.

REPORTER. Well please, just pretend I'm not here. I'll just sit and observe if that's all right. *(Beat.)*

SOLOMON. The three of us were just practicing Lincoln/Douglas debate.

DIWATA. *(To Solomon.)* Lincoln/Douglas is two people.

HOWIE. Would you be able to come back at another time? We're working out some rough spots, you know?

REPORTER. Oh. Well …

SOLOMON. Yeah, I'm sorry, it's just, we're just a mess right now.

REPORTER. Is there a particular rehearsal I should attend, or…?

DIWATA. You should come back and see us do Group Interpretation.

REPORTER. What's Group Interpretation?

DIWATA. It's a category in which all three of us come together to tell a story. It's the only one we do together.

REPORTER. What story will you be telling?

HOWIE. Not now …   SOLOMON. No, Diwata …

DIWATA. We can tell any story we like, a fairy tale, a fable, a legend … but we've decided to tell *our* story. The story of how we came together.

REPORTER. Well, that's the story I'm hoping to capture. I cover the regional beat on the local NPR station — this is exactly the kind of story they love to air.

DIWATA. You mean it would be read on the radio? Amazing …

REPORTER. Well, not so amazing — it would just be me reading a shortened version of the article I'd put together for the *Oregonian*.

DIWATA. Could I read it? I'm amazing at voiceovers.

REPORTER. Well, no — the journalists read their own reports —

DIWATA. I could *play* you. Could I play you?

SOLOMON. No, Diwata.   HOWIE. Diwata, pull back.

REPORTER. I'm hoping to get this in the Sunday broadcast, so, the sooner you guys can tell me your story the better.

DIWATA. It's going to be pretty controversial, just to warn you.

SOLOMON. Diwata …

DIWATA. *(To Solomon.)* I didn't tell her anything …

REPORTER. What's controversial about it? *(Howie jumps in before Diwata can speak.)*

HOWIE. The rules of Group Interpretation say that you can't use costumes or props. *(Beat.)* And we use costumes and props. And that's going to be pretty controversial.

REPORTER. I see.

DIWATA. Dancing isn't allowed either, but I simply couldn't resist using the very special dance moves that Howard is going to teach us.

HOWIE. Jesus Christ …

REPORTER. What type of dance?

DIWATA. Striptease. Mainly. *(Aside, to Solomon.)* I still have my bodystocking. *(Solomon buries his head in his hands.)*

REPORTER. *(Laughing.)* That does sound controversial. And what is the significance of all this dancing?

DIWATA. Well Jan, besides finally having a platform for my ten years of jazz/modern dance — the significance of the striptease is to show that, as we shed our clothing, we are baring, via metaphorical conceit … baring our … bathing suit areas, which is the term from stranger-danger, the one they use in place of penis and vagina. The piece is inspired by each of our original flows — a mashing together of each of our voices.

HOWIE. Mostly hers.

REPORTER. *(Taking out her notepad.)* And so, explain to me the whole bathing suit business again?

SOLOMON. She means, it's like, we're showing people that ready or not —

DIWATA. Here come our bathing suit areas. *(Solomon and Howie stare at Diwata.)*

SOLOMON. Please don't talk. *(To the Reporter.)* We're showing people that ready or not, we're going to discuss things that are affecting us in real terms, adult terms, and we won't apologize even if it makes you uncomfortable.

HOWIE. And my moves aren't that special. Just a disclaimer.

DIWATA. He's just nervous people will laugh at him. Childhood trauma.

SOLOMON. *(To Reporter.)* I'm really sorry about this …

REPORTER. Not at all, this is quite good timing, really — I'm writing a new foreword to my book — it deals with adolescence, how kids like you often form your own clusters apart from adults; and the formation of your group — I think it would be the perfect new beginning, capturing the image of you three performing this group event — what is it called?

DIWATA. Group Interpretation.

REPORTER. Could I stop by sometime before Friday? Just to see even a rough rehearsal? You'd be doing me a huge favor. I'd speak to your parents of course to make sure this was okay.

DIWATA. What do we get out of it?

SOLOMON. Diwata … *(To the Reporter.)* I'm sorry.

REPORTER. It's fine, it's a fair question. *(Beat.)* Other than an appearance in the *Oregonian*, I'm not sure what else I have to offer. *(Beat.)*

DIWATA. Is your sister-in-law still on the board of the Salem dinner theatre? I googled you, so … sorry if that's weird.

SOLOMON. Yes, it is weird, Diwata.

HOWIE. *(To the Reporter.)* She's an actress.

REPORTER. *(To Diwata.)* I could certainly introduce you, if you like.

SOLOMON. That isn't necessary, we're not asking you for any favors.

HOWIE. *(To the Reporter.)* Do you know anyone in town who might be willing to serve as an advisor for the Gay/Straight Alliance at school? I've been looking for someone for over a month, but …

SOLOMON. Howie …

REPORTER. Well, certainly no promises, but I might be able to help.

SOLOMON. Again, there's no way we could be ready in time.

REPORTER. Solomon, your father told me about the article you wrote for the school paper. No promises, but there's a chance we could find a place for it in the *Oregonian*. *(All three look at each other. Introduction to George Michael's "Freedom" sounds.* Blackout.)*

Scene 9: Group Interpretation

The music continues from the previous scene.

The dance should primarily be just that — a choreographed dance, with dance moves. It should loosely convey the following story:

Diwata enters, "dances" her blog using some very basic jazz/ modern dance moves. She is totally serious about all of this.

Howie enters, somewhat reluctantly, and after receiving a signal from Diwata, does some of his very special moves. Diwata joins in.

Howie and Diwata look for Solomon to enter. He doesn't. Diwata exits, quickly returns pushing Solomon onstage.

Howie and Solomon flank Diwata and each pull one of her

---

* See Special Note on Songs and Recordings on copyright page.

arms — they are fighting for control of her. They move one way, then move the other way — Diwata is very dramatic about all of this.

Diwata does a grand move (i.e., a lift, or stage diving from a desk into the boys' arms). It's awkward for the boys, but she maintains full stage presence. Her moves grow in intensity and difficulty, and it becomes clear she has choreographed the dance to make herself the center of attention. She uses the boys as tools for her more complex moves.

And then, in time with the music ...

Diwata removes a piece of clothing.

And then another.

And another.

Diwata is wearing nothing but a nude bodystocking. She is in heaven.

Howie and Solomon follow her lead, removing their clothing, a bit less enthusiastically. Howie is getting a kick out of the proceedings ... and even Solomon relaxes (just a bit) as the music reaches its infectious climax.

The boys have on poorly dyed flesh-colored baggy T-shirts and boxers.

With a flourish, they finish. A tympani/cymbal crash sounds in time with a sharp blackout.

Scene 10: Oral Interpretation of Prose

(Note: Scene 10 may be cut at the discretion of the producing theater. It was included in the initial New York production, but was cut in the subsequent Chicago production.)

Howie, Solomon, and Diwata are each in their bedrooms, listening to the radio broadcast.

RADIO HOST. *(Voiceover.)* "The mayor may not be granting interviews, but three local students are talking about the biggest political scandal in Oregon's history. The newly-formed Speech & Debate team at North Salem High School, led by team captain Diwanda Jones —"

SOLOMON. Team captain?

DIWATA. Diwanda?

RADIO HOST. *(Voiceover.)* "— is attempting to explore the ins and outs of the sex scandal and other taboo topics using the various Speech & Debate categories in unconventional and creative ways …"

SOLOMON. Good, solid …

RADIO HOST. *(Voiceover.)* Regional Beat reporter Jan Clark sat in on a recent rehearsal of the team and had a chance to speak with Salem's young oratorical pioneers.

REPORTER. *(Voiceover.)* The rehearsal I attended was anything but ordinary …

DIWATA. That's right …

REPORTER. *(Voiceover.)* Up first was a wild dance fantasia in which the kids removed their clothing to reveal that each of them was wearing beige undergarments …

DIWATA. *(Disappointed.)* She didn't get the metaphor … oh, Jan …

REPORTER. *(Voiceover.)* … a self-professed symbol of their struggles to bare their souls to an adult community who rarely takes the time to listen …

HOWIE. Please call her "Diwanda" again. Please …

REPORTER. *(Voiceover.)* A more detailed description of the scene will make an appearance in the new forward to my book, *Adolescents*

Alone, now in its eighth printing at Simon & Schuster.

DIWATA. She's plugging her book?

REPORTER. *(Voiceover.)* As I note in my book ... *(Diwata gives the radio the finger.)* ... kids of this generation have a tendency to search out a safe place, an escape from their loneliness, forming small complex clusters of friends to help navigate the complex world of high school together.

SOLOMON. Friends?

DIWATA. No, we're not —

REPORTER. *(Voiceover.)* ... Even as I wandered North Salem's halls, I was hit with my own fears and insecurities. I was also hit with the frighteningly familiar smells of the cafeteria, that odd scent of Pine-Sol mingling with rotting food ...

SOLOMON. That would be my vomit.

REPORTER. *(Voiceover.)* ... and as I sat in the classroom, I was once again reminded of the simple truth: Adolescents crave meaningful relationships with adults who care about them.

VOICE (DIWATA'S MOTHER). Diwata ...

DIWATA. *(Yelling.)* Mother, please die so you will be dead. *God.*

REPORTER. *(Voiceover.)* That is an oversimplification of my own argument, which is thoroughly fleshed out in my book, *Adolescents Alone*, published by Simon and Schuster.

DIWATA. Stop plugging your book, Jan.

REPORTER. *(Voiceover.)* And as for Solomon, Howard, and Diwanda ...

DIWATA. Oh, c'mon!

HOWIE. *(Loving the mistake.)* Yes ...

REPORTER. *(Voiceover.)* ... at present, their work may not be particularly ground-breaking ...

HOWIE/DIWATA/SOLOMON. Ouch/Bitch/Owww ...

REPORTER. *(Voiceover.)* ... and if their writing or performing does not show prodigious skill ...

HOWIE/DIWATA/SOLOMON. Ouch/Slut/Ohhhh ...

REPORTER. *(Voiceover.)* ... someday soon this dynamic trio will be ready to share their performance with us; and when they are, I encourage you to show up with an open mind. If you go to listen, you will leave talking.

RADIO HOST. *(Voiceover.)* Jan Clark will be reading from her book, *Adolescents Alone*, at Barnes & Noble this Saturday at one P.M.

HOWIE/SOLOMON. Pathetic ... /Unbelievable ...

DIWATA. Media whore … *(Blackout.)*

Scene 11: Student Congress

A sign that reads: Welcome to the 1st Meeting of North Salem's Gay/Straight Alliance!

Howie, Diwata, and Solomon are seated. They look towards the door, their silence upstaged by the sign.

Howie checks to see if anyone else is coming.

DIWATA. How weird is it if we are the only members of the Speech & Debate team and the Gay/Straight Alliance? *(Howie throws something at Diwata.)*
HOWIE. It's already after three, I guess we should start. First on the agenda is meet-and-greet, introductions.
SOLOMON. *(Introducing himself to Diwata.)* Hi, I'm Solomon …
DIWATA. *(Teasing.)* Oh, hi — we actually met in the third-floor bathroom last year …
HOWIE. Okay, enough …
SOLOMON. That's disgusting.
HOWIE. I'm sure more people will come once the word gets out.
SOLOMON. My parents think I'm doing community service.
DIWATA. How are Mary and Joseph?
SOLOMON. That's not funny. They're shipping me out to Exodus again for their spring seminar.
DIWATA. Yikes.
SOLOMON. We've got like, a family therapist now though, and she made them promise to not send me again if it doesn't work out.
HOWIE. That's some progress, yes?
SOLOMON. Uh, some, yeah …
DIWATA. *(Raising her hand.)* Oh, oh — can I put something on the agenda — the dates I'm going on for the Salem Dinner Theatre production of *Fiddler on the Roof*? The theater is gay-friendly, it's relevant.
HOWIE. That's fine, Diwata.
SOLOMON. How's that going?

DIWATA. I'm the standby for all the daughters. I have to serve drinks at intermission right now, which sucks, but I'm going on the twentieth. Shprintze is having her wisdom teeth out.

SOLOMON. Nice.

HOWIE. Duly noted — *(Loud knocking on the door.)* Come on in ... *(Howie goes to the door, looks.)* There's no one there. That's weird.

DIWATA. Ohmigod, we have a gay ghost. I love it.

HOWIE. It's Mr. Healy, haunting us ...

SOLOMON. That's not funny.

DIWATA. Healy's come to offer handjobs to all incoming students.

SOLOMON. Stop it. *(More knocking at the door.)* Come in!

VOICE #1. *(From offstage.)*   VOICE #2. *(From offstage.)*
You guys want to   Fucking faggots!
give me head, cocksuckers! ...

(From offstage the sound of laughter and kids running away. Beat. Howie goes to the door, looks.)

HOWIE. *(Looking outside the door.)* It's your mom and dad, Solomon. *(Howie and Diwata laugh.)*

SOLOMON. Do you think — you don't think they heard what we were talking about, do you?

DIWATA. No, no —

HOWIE. We didn't say anything specific about Mr. Healy, we just — no, I'm sure we didn't.

SOLOMON. Diwata said about — you heard what she said.

DIWATA. No one would know what that meant, it was a generic remark, *God. (Beat.)*

SOLOMON. Well ... should we keep going, or...?

DIWATA. Yes, what's next?

HOWIE. Election of officers. There are four positions open, so ... guess we save that for next meeting, when the word spreads.

SOLOMON. Definitely.

HOWIE. And that's it.

SOLOMON. Okay.

DIWATA. Good.

HOWIE. Meeting adjourned.

DIWATA. I gotta go upload another video podcast to my website before 'mah fans get upset ...

HOWIE. Your last one had, like, three hits.

DIWATA. All viral videos start from a small place, Howard. Later ladies ... *(Diwata exits.)*

HOWIE. They didn't hear us.

SOLOMON. You don't know that.

HOWIE. What if they did? I mean … what if they did?

SOLOMON. I don't know what she saw … I don't know if Diwata told you details or … if she said I was the one who, you know …

HOWIE. What does it matter?

SOLOMON. Yeah, well … because I'm not telling people that. *(Howie gathers his things, starts to exit.)* Hey, maybe we could hang out sometime, like for real, you know?

HOWIE. As friends, yeah — of course —

SOLOMON. Sure, of course as friends. Of course as *friends*.

HOWIE. I think it's clear you need a Christian hottie, you know?

SOLOMON. Dude, of course. Yes. Cool. I'm gonna find like a million at Exodus.

HOWIE. No, I know, I know.

SOLOMON. Definitely, awesome then. Well then, really cool then, we'll talk soon. *(Howie sees Solomon is defeated — calls to him before he can exit.)*

HOWIE. Yeah, and I did go to the park that night to meet Healy. *(Howie continues to gather his things.)*

SOLOMON. You said you didn't.

HOWIE. I didn't meet him … but … because he never showed up. Guess he didn't like my pic. I shouldn't have said I was a blond. *(Stops, sees Solomon isn't smiling.)* I'm kidding.

SOLOMON. So —

HOWIE. I'm just telling you, I don't want to talk about it.

SOLOMON. No. I don't either. *(Howie exits. Blackout.)*

Scene 12: Original Oratory

Diwata is alone in her bedroom creating her latest podcast. Music underscores her speech.

DIWATA. Right now, the overture is striking up for North Salem High's final dress rehearsal of *Once Upon a Mattress*. Sadly, I am not participating in this year's show due to miscasting. For weeks now, I

pondered revenge, especially after meeting two lovely young ladies, two girly fans who loved my blog … *(Lights up on Howie and Solomon in separate rooms listening to her blog broadcast with headphones.)* HOWIE. Oh, she's dead.   SOLOMON. I'm going to kill her …
DIWATA. … but then I stopped and asked myself: Diwata, what would Jesus do? What would Mary do? And then I thought … *(She stops the music.)* … what would Mary Rodgers do? *(She starts the music again, turns up the volume on her Casio keyboard. A funkier vamp continues under the following …)* I wondered: What would the organization in charge of licensing the rights to *Once Upon a Mattress* do? So I called and asked them. Imagine my surprise when I was informed that if any changes were made to the script without proper consent … a representative from the Rodgers & Hammerstein Organization would fly out, see the show; and if what I reported proved to be correct … the show would be shut down. *(Howie and Solomon react.)*
HOWIE. No, she didn't …   SOLOMON. Oh God …
DIWATA. This is all purely hypothetical, of course. Still … if I were you, I wouldn't buy my tickets in advance. Rest in peace Mary … whether it be in a grave or on your living room couch. This flow's for you. *(Singing.)*
        Oh … oh …
Sing it with me now …
HOWIE.
        Oh … oh …
DIWATA and SOLOMON. *(Simultaneous with Howie.)*
        Oh-ee, oh-ee …
DIWATA. Take it home now …
        Yadda-da-da …
SOLOMON. *(Simultaneous with above.)*
        Oh-ee … oh-ee …
HOWIE. *(Simultaneous with above.)*
        Oh … oh …
VOICE (DIWATA'S MOTHER). Hey, hey, hey … keep it down. *(Diwata turns her Casio off, the singing stops.)*
DIWATA. Signing off for the last time. Good night. *(Lights fade on Diwata.)*
HOWIE. G'night … *(The lights fade on Howie. Solomon is alone in his bedroom in front of his laptop. He types a message. It is projected as in the first scene. His screen name is "Abe16.")*

ABE16:   im new to this chat room
            gay/wmale/16

(Beat. He types again.)

ABE16:   anyone out there?

(Beat. He stares at the screen, waits. A tympani roll accompanies a sharp blackout.)

End of Play

PRODUCTION NOTES

Opening I.M. Scene

The Quicktime movie of the I.M. chat (Scene 1) that DPS has made available is a mock-up I created for the first workshop production. The timing of the I.M. text in this mock-up corresponds to a specific version of Aaron Copland's *Fanfare for the Common Man* (from the album *Copland Conducts Copland* — Columbia Symphony Orchestra — Record label: Sony Classical). (A way to know if you're a bit off: The first four tympani crashes match up exactly with the first four lines of I.M. text, and the fifth line, "LOL," corresponds with the first entrance of the trumpets).

Song Choice in Scene 9: GROUP INTERPRETATION

The song *Freedom* was used in the original production, with the scene ending around 2:40 into the track. The entire scene shouldn't be any longer than 3 minutes.

Music

The sheet music and corresponding background tracks are pretty self-explanatory. Let me add the following notes:

The songs are all sung in a pop-music style. Accordingly, the rhythms on the sheet music are not precisely accurate ... just very, very close. The teaching tracks on the CD should clarify this. Also, AEA rules forbade me from including tracks of the original cast members singing the songs. Instead, you get my voice. I'm so sorry.

A note to all future Diwatas: do not attempt to sing poorly. That's not the point. My illustrious score will take care of the less laudable aspects of Diwata's music ... you can't sound too good. As far as I'm concerned, Diwata can have a killer voice. Sing her songs sincerely — like you were singing a piece of music that you truly respect. That's the point.

The background tracks are mandatory simply because Diwata is working with a used, low-end Casio keyboard. The accompaniments shouldn't be dressed up or played live — even if your theater has a baby-grand waiting in the wings. We should always believe that her not-so-grand keyboard is generating the accompaniments.

Intermission/Scene Changes

The play should be performed without an intermission. That said, the play should also not run longer that 100 minutes.

Note to Actors/Directors

I learned a lot about the nuances of this play over the course of auditions and the first incarnations of the play, so (at the risk of stating the obvious), I wanted to pass along the following advice:

Actors, I ask that you not only avoid playing for laughs, but also avoid playing young, playing gay, playing nerdy, playing a deranged diva ... you get the point. Trust that the language will craft the characters' outsider traits. If the performances feel too broad to stand alone in front of a silent audience ... then, in my opinion, the performances are too broad. The moment you feel you are too "normal" to play one of these parts and dress up the role with lots of ticks and affects, the play loses its maximum effect. The more honestly these characters are portrayed, the richer (and funnier) the play becomes.

— S.A.K.
February, 2008

Monoblog

Stephen Karam

(the labelled parts--A, B, C, D--represent the four accompaniment tracks that are used during the song.)

Sit-ing at my Ca - si-o key-board

Thank God it's built - to pre-re-co - rd o-ther wise I____ could'-nt play and sing

2006

Monoblog

Diwata: at the same time – I – ee-I-ee-I'm sit-ing at my Ca-si-o key-board

Diwata: Kin-da drunk and re – ly fu-ckin' bo – red o-ther wise I'd –

Diwata: – have bet-ter things to do then up-date my blog____ on a Fri-day night

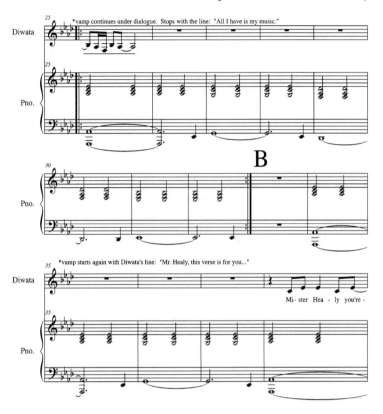

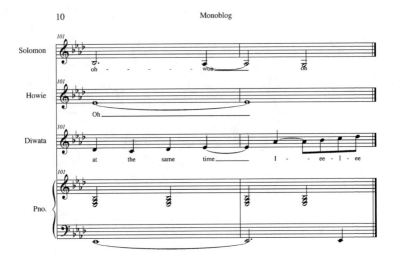

Hold It In

Stephen Karam

2006

this is Sa-lem I just - had my tri-al they think - I'm a witch they think -

- I'm vi - le They - said girl you'll hang you must - con - fess - so I -

Hold It In

Diwata: Hold it in ___
Howie: I should ___ 'nt tell ___

Diwata: Not on your life   Just hold it in ___
Howie: ___ them?   But they'll still   love me.

Hold It In

Hold It In

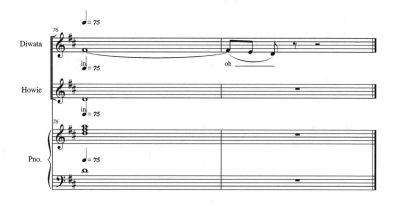

Finale (pt. 2 - vocal)

Stephen Karam

2006

PROPERTY LIST

Laptop computers
Papers
Tape recorder
Newspaper
Empty wine coolers (4)
Headphones (2)
Cell phones (3)
School bag with papers
iPhone
Business card
Chat transcript
Coffee pot, mug
Dish towel
Plate of fries
Rule book
Index card
Trash can
Tissues
Notepad, pen

NEW PLAYS

★ **AGES OF THE MOON by Sam Shepard.** Byron and Ames are old friends, reunited by mutual desperation. Over bourbon on ice, they sit, reflect and bicker until fifty years of love, friendship and rivalry are put to the test at the barrel of a gun. "A poignant and honest continuation of themes that have always been present in the work of one of this country's most important dramatists, here reconsidered in the light and shadow of time passed." –NY Times. "Finely wrought...as enjoyable and enlightening as a night spent stargazing." –Talkin' Broadway. [2M] ISBN: 978-0-8222-2462-4

★ **ALL THE WAY by Robert Schenkkan. Winner of the 2014 Tony Award for Best Play.** November, 1963. An assassin's bullet catapults Lyndon Baines Johnson into the presidency. A Shakespearean figure of towering ambition and appetite, this charismatic, conflicted Texan hurls himself into the passage of the Civil Rights Act—a tinderbox issue emblematic of a divided America—even as he campaigns for re-election in his own right, and the recognition he so desperately wants. In Pulitzer Prize and Tony Award–winning Robert Schenkkan's vivid dramatization of LBJ's first year in office, means versus ends plays out on the precipice of modern America. ALL THE WAY is a searing, enthralling exploration of the morality of power. It's not personal, it's just politics. "...action-packed, thoroughly gripping... jaw-dropping political drama." –Variety. "A theatrical coup...nonstop action. The suspense of a first-class thriller." –NY1. [17M, 3W] ISBN: 978-0-8222-3181-3

★ **CHOIR BOY by Tarell Alvin McCraney.** The Charles R. Drew Prep School for Boys is dedicated to the creation of strong, ethical black men. Pharus wants nothing more than to take his rightful place as leader of the school's legendary gospel choir. Can he find his way inside the hallowed halls of this institution if he sings in his own key? "[An] affecting and honest portrait...of a gay youth tentatively beginning to find the courage to let the truth about himself become known." –NY Times. "In his stirring and stylishly told drama, Tarell Alvin McCraney cannily explores race and sexuality and the graces and gravity of history." –NY Daily News. [7M] ISBN: 978-0-8222-3116-5

★ **THE ELECTRIC BABY by Stefanie Zadravec.** When Helen causes a car accident that kills a young man, a group of fractured souls cross paths and connect around a mysterious dying baby who glows like the moon. Folk tales and folklore weave throughout this magical story of sad endings, strange beginnings and the unlikely people that get you from one place to the next. "The imperceptible magic that pervades human existence and the power of myth to assuage sorrow are invoked by the playwright as she entwines the lives of strangers in THE ELECTRIC BABY, a touching drama." –NY Times. "As dazzling as the dialogue is dreamful." –Pittsburgh City Paper. [3M, 3W] ISBN: 978-0-8222-3011-3

DRAMATISTS PLAY SERVICE, INC.
440 Park Avenue South, New York, NY 10016 212-683-8960 Fax 212-213-1539
postmaster@dramatists.com www.dramatists.com